Industrial Purchasing Behavior

Industrial Purchasing Behavior

A Study of Communications Effects

THEODORE LEVITT

Professor of Business Administration

HF5437
. L66

69366

RELEASE
ST. JOSEPH'S UNIVERSITY   STX
HF5437.L66
Industrial purchasing behavior ;

3 9353 00089 7502

DIVISION OF RESEARCH

GRADUATE SCHOOL OF BUSINESS ADMINISTRATION

HARVARD UNIVERSITY

Boston · 1965

Foreword

THE RESEARCH reported here is related to a broader program of research in marketing which is going forward at this School. This broader program has several distinguishing features. Its most general characteristic is to view customers as people solving problems, and hence an emphasis on customer or buyer "decision making." It has long been a matter of practical knowledge and concern that buying decisions involve large elements of risk and uncertainty, and this feature of decision making—the handling of risk and uncertainty—is a central focus of this program. A second characteristic is that the approach to the risk and uncertainty elements is partly from the point of view of statistical decision theory and partly from communication theory in the behavioral sciences. Decision theory has suggested ways of looking systematically at risk reduction in buying as well as other decisions, and communication theory has suggested the many ways in which the buying audience is affected by selling communications in practical marketing efforts.

This particular project involved an experiment which attempted to simulate in as natural a fashion as possible some of the basic factors involved in a sales presentation of an industrial materials salesman to prospective purchasers. The experiment itself was carefully designed to test the applicability to purchasing decisions of concepts taken from communication theory and to distinguish among the effects on various purchasing groups of the many aspects of the selling communication. For example, what relevance are the reputation of the company selling the product, the quality of the selling presentation, and the skill of the salesman, for what kind of purchasing group, and for what type of purchasing decisions?

The differential effects revealed by the experiment show the relevance to marketing managers of the varied elements of selling efforts, and how they need to be considered in the formulation of marketing strategy. The study will also suggest to other researchers significant new avenues for further inquiry.

For the School, I want to express appreciation to the Celanese Corporation of America for a special grant for this research and to The Associates of the Harvard Business School whose generous gifts contributed the major support for this project.

BERTRAND FOX
Director of Research

Soldiers Field
Boston, Massachusetts
October 1965

Author's Acknowledgments

THIS BOOK is an outgrowth of the inspiration, guidance, and continuing counsel of my colleague, Professor Raymond A. Bauer. Without him the present study would not have been undertaken and could not possibly have whatever merits it does. While his help has been invaluable, he has had those rare qualities of restraint and encouragement which enables me now to give him all possible credit for the merits the study may have while fully freeing him of its shortcomings, errors, misinterpretations, and perhaps even muddleheadedness.

The study was undertaken with the generous financial support of the many individual and company supporters of The Associates of the Harvard Business School and a special grant from the Celanese Corporation of America. I wish also to thank Professor Bertrand Fox, Director of the Division of Research, for his very careful reading of the manuscript at two stages and his exceedingly helpful comments and suggestions. Miss Ruth Norton, Editor and Executive Secretary of the Division of Research, was very helpful in preparing the manuscript for publication.

Mr. George Gibson, Director of the Harvard Business School's Audio-Visual Center, and Mr. Sam Zanghi, Assistant Director, were very helpful and generous with their time and professional guidance in the preparation of the sales simulation script and movies. My colleague, Professor Wilbur B. England, was also exceedingly helpful in conceptualizing the study, reading and commenting on the manuscript, and in obtaining the invaluable cooperation of Mr. Eliot P. Emerson of the New England Purchasing Agents Association, Inc. Also helpful was Mr. James J. Jagger, Vice President of Arthur D. Little, Inc., Cambridge, Massachusetts, in arranging for the participation of his company's technical personnel in the study. Mrs. Bertha Daniels of the Harvard Business School's Data Processing Bureau was continuously helpful in every respect.

I am also indebted to Mr. Owen J. Brown, Marketing Vice President of Cabot Corporation, and to Mr. Albert F. Steffen and Mr. Henry P. Donohue, Jr., also of Cabot, for their invaluable assistance in developing materials which were used in conducting the study.

Finally, I owe a very special and deep gratitude to two former students who did nearly all the data processing and much of the presentational conceptualizing that has resulted in the data format used in this book. But far beyond that, they did a great deal of highly perceptive and original analytical work and they did it with surprising economy of time, wonderful cheerfulness, and uncommon dedication and good sense. These two invaluable assistants are Mr. Ronald Demer, now with Keydata Corporation, Cambridge, Massachusetts, and Mr. Robert L. Yohe, now with Hooker Chemical Corp. in New Orleans, Louisiana.

A listing of indebtedness in a project that involved as many persons as the present one almost inevitably looks encyclopedic and therefore undiscriminating. But appearances in this case are wrong. If anything, the list is too brief. Added to it belong at least four other important names—Dean George P. Baker and Associate Dean George F. F. Lombard of the Harvard Business School, both of whose kindly and gentle encouragement and whose special arrangements of my School affairs never escaped me; Mrs. Priscilla L. Chamberlin, whose secretarial and administrative talents kept things going with efficient smoothness; and my wife, Joan, whose cheerful and unobtrusive managerial activities back at the ranch created the needed environment and time to carry out the entire task.

Although many persons obviously contributed greatly toward making this study possible, it should be clear that none of them are in any way responsible for its findings, interpretations, errors, or for the research methods employed. These are my own sole responsibility. I accept it gladly but with gratitude for all that others have contributed.

THEODORE LEVITT

Boston, Massachusetts
September 1965

Contents

List of Exhibits

CHAPTER 1

Introduction:
The Problem and the Study

ONE OF THE venerable questions in marketing, and particularly the marketing of industrial products, is whether a company's generalized reputation affects its ability to sell its products. With the great flood of new products in recent years, the question has been focused more sharply around the extent to which a company's generalized reputation affects its ability to launch new products. While nobody claims that a good reputation is an adequate substitute for a good product supported by a good sales effort, the question remains as to what contribution a good reputation can make to a successful selling effort. Thus, all other things being equal, does a relatively well-known company such as DuPont have a real edge over a relatively obscure company? Would it pay for a relatively obscure company to spend more money to advertise and promote its name and general competence or to spend more on training its salesmen?

These are some of the questions to which this monograph is addressed. The monograph reports on a study conducted by the author at the Graduate School of Business Administration, Harvard University. The method of the study, which is reported in detail in Chapter 3, is an outgrowth and elaboration of methods developed by behavioral scientists studying the psychology of propaganda and communication. The central piece of modern research on this subject was published in 1951 by Hovland and Weiss in their now-famous article on

"The Influence of Source Credibility on Communication Effectiveness." [1]

THE PSYCHOLOGY OF COMMUNICATION

The article demonstrated that the ability of a message to influence or persuade its audience is related to the credibility of the message source. Thus a newspaper editorial identified to one group of Americans as emanating, say, from *The New York Times* and to another group of Americans as emanating, say, from *Pravda* would, on the basis of the Hovland-Weiss findings, lead one to expect that a change in audience opinion in the direction advocated by the editorial would be greater for those who believed it was a *New York Times* editorial than those who believed it to be a *Pravda* editorial. In other words, the audience's feelings about the credibility of the message source helped determine the persuasive effectiveness of the message itself: the greater the prestige or the more believable the message source, the more likely that it will influence the audience in the direction advocated by the message. The less prestigeful or believable the source, the less likely that it will influence the audience in the direction advocated by the message. This phenomenon is now generally referred to as the "source effect."

The Hovland-Weiss article revived an interest in an area of communications research that had existed in American universities nearly a generation before and had actually been modestly rekindled by the publication two years earlier of *Experiments in Mass Communication* by Hovland, Lumsdaine, and Sheffield.[2] This latter publication not only re-affirmed

---

[1] Carl I. Hovland and Walter Weiss, "The Influence of Source Credibility on Communication Effectiveness," 1951. (For complete publishing data, see Bibliography.)

[2] Carl I. Hovland, Arthur A. Lumsdaine, and Fred D. Sheffield, *Experiments in Mass Communication,* 1949.

earlier findings [3, 4] of a connection between source credibility and audience attitude change, but it went further. It established a paradoxical connection between source credibility and the duration of attitude change over time. Previous published research on message durability had been confined to learning situations. It had demonstrated the existence of a "forgetting curve" [5]—namely, that the retention of learned information or facts generally declines with the passage of time. Hence it might have been expected that attitude changes produced by a message that communicated certain facts would be moderated as the retention of these facts declined over time. But the experiments of Hovland, Lumsdaine, and Sheffield discovered that an over-time decline in the retention of factual learned material by an audience could be accompanied during that period by an increase or strengthening of that audience's attitude change toward the subject matter to which the learned facts referred. This unexpected result, which the authors referred to as "sleeper effect," raised profound questions about communications phenomena. Hovland detailed these questions and in 1951 laid out a program of research designed to help answer them. [6] A considerable outpouring of research followed, much of which Hovland himself initiated and carried out. Almost simultaneously with this 1951 call for research came the Hovland-Weiss article on "The Influence of Source Credibility on Communication Effectiveness."

The research reported in this article demonstrated that while there was no difference in factual information retention as between audiences exposed to what can be classified as a

---

[3] Mitchel Saadi and Paul R. Farnsworth, "The Degrees of Acceptance of Dogmatic Statements and Preferences for Their Supposed Makers," 1934.

[4] A. O. Bowden, Floyd F. Caldwell, and Guy A. West, "A Study in Prestige," 1934.

[5] Alfred G. Dietze and George E. Jones, "Factual Memory of Secondary School Pupils for a Short Article Which They Read a Single Time," 1931.

[6] Carl I. Hovland, "Changes in Attitude Through Communication," 1951.

high-trust, high-credibility source versus those exposed to
what can be classified as a low-trust, low-credibility source,
there were statistically significant changes in audience opinion
changes. The high-trust, high-credibility source produced significantly more opinion change in the direction it advocated
than the low-trust, low-credibility source. These results were
based on measures taken immediately after all the audiences
were exposed to the identical messages. On a re-test four
weeks later, sleeper effect showed up. Opinion change among
audiences which had been exposed to the high-credibility
source was now less than in the immediately-after measure
four weeks earlier, and among those exposed to the low-credibility source it was now more than before. In 1953 Weiss published experimental results which provided even stronger evidence of the power of this sleeper effect and the role of source
credibility.[7] The results suggested that the cause of sleeper
effect was either the result of the audience over time forgetting
the source more quickly than the material that was presented,
thus enabling the material that was still retained to be more
persuasive, or it was the result of a less spontaneous association of the message content with the source, with the same
effect. In any case, it was shown that the degree of retention of
the factual material learned was not the cause of the sleeper
effect.

Also in 1953 Kelman and Hovland published research [8] suggesting that credibility is not just a function of the generalized
reputation for trustworthiness that attaches to a source, but
also a function of the audience's feelings about the source's
competence to speak on a subject. A high-competence source
is a high-credibility source, and a low-competence source is
a low-credibility source. The results of this experiment were
the same as those using generalized credibility as a means of

---

[7] Walter Weiss, "A 'Sleeper' Effect in Opinion Change," 1953.

[8] Herman C. Kelman and Carl I. Hovland, " 'Reinstatement' of the
Communicator in Delayed Measurement of Opinion Change," 1953.

distinguishing between sources. The research also showed that when, with the passage of time, respondents are reminded of the sources of the messages to which they were originally exposed (i.e., "source reinstatement"), the acceptance of the viewpoint of the high-competence source rose above the non-reinstated level and that of the low-competence source fell.

A subsequent summary of the results of this study in *Communication and Persuasion* by Hovland, Janis, and Kelley made an observation that catapulted later research into profoundly important new areas. The summary said in part:

> In the Kelman and Hovland study, recall for items on the communication was determined at the delayed after-test. Here again there was no significant difference between the positive [high-credibility] and the negative [low-credibility] sources. An interesting incidental finding was that *recall was significantly better when the communication was given by a neutral source than either the positive or negative source.* The authors suggest that affective response may adversely influence the amount of material learned and recalled, and that both the positive and negative communicators were responded to with greater affect than the neutral one. *An emotional reaction to the communicator may focus attention upon him to the detriment of attending to his conclusions and learning his arguments.* This result indicates, as we would expect, that there are some instances in which *the communicator affects the degree to which the content is acquired.*[9]

In other words, in addition to the source effect and the sleeper effect, there may be two other critical communications "effect": "communicator effect" (as distinguished from "source"), and "audience effect." Bauer first raised the issue of the role of the audience itself in his 1958 article on "The Communicator and the Audience." [10] In a paper delivered at

---

[9] Carl I. Hovland, Irving L. Janis, and Harold K. Kelley, *Communication and Persuasion*, 1953. Italics added.

[10] Raymond A. Bauer, "The Communicator and the Audience," 1958.

a meeting of the New England Psychological Association in 1962 he discussed his theme more fully under the title "The Initiative of the Audience." He specifically raised the question of "what the audience was trying to accomplish in the situation" that is under scrutiny, and how this affects communication. Referring to the Maccobys' studies on homeostatic theory in attitude change,[11] he pointed out that "audiences typically strive to maintain some sort of equilibrium in their belief structure . . ." and are therefore "positively motivated to maintain the existing state in many instances. . . ." In partial further support of his point that the audience is an active agent in the communications transaction to a degree which must be treated with the greatest research care, he noted how Hovland himself had shown "that the effects achieved [in his studies] . . . were a function of the way in which audiences were active in defining the credibility they attributed to the source."

The specific area in which this "initiative of the audience" has been particularly well demonstrated is in situations in which audience opinion and attitude change involve high degrees of risk for the audience. Thus physicians considering the use of a new drug for the first time may be faced with a very risky decision. Bauer has shown,[12] by reference both to his own research and to that of others, that "as the riskiness of the decision increases . . . doctors are progressively and strongly more selective in their use of the sources" whose word they will take regarding the appropriateness of prescribing a given drug.

That there are risk elements in drug prescription may be easy enough to see and accept. Hence it is relatively easy to accept the concept of the "initiative of the audience" in such

---

[11] Nathan Maccoby and Eleanor E. Maccoby, "Homeostatic Theory in Attitude Change," 1961.

[12] Raymond A. Bauer, "Risk Handling in Drug Adoption: The Role of Company Preference," 1961.

situations. But research by Cox [13] demonstrates that the initiative and role of the audience apply even in such presumably mundane areas as consumers buying nylon stockings. And the audience takes a certain initiative not simply to reduce dissonnance. The stocking buyer has selection "problems." She takes a certain routine initiative in solving these problems. The character of that initiative can be multivaried, and can depend not just on what is at stake in terms of money or suitability. Her generalized self-confidence, Cox found, is a vital factor in the "initiative" she takes. This in turn affects the effectiveness of sales and advertising communications directed at her.

But beyond that, it also affects the communicator who, taking his cues from the audience, arranges his communications in ways designed to be more effective with the audience. The fields of advertising and sales promotion have become increasingly preoccupied in the last two decades with the importance of such cues in the development of their sales messages and the selection of the media through which these are communicated. The obvious evidence of this rising preoccupation is the explosive growth of consumer research as a business function, as a profession, and as a formal course offered in universities. Business studies its audiences increasingly more in order to communicate with them increasingly more effectively.

Yet research into the communications process has, according to Bauer, in one respect lagged behind what communications practitioners seem widely to assume is an important element of communication. This is what Bauer calls the "transactional" character of communications.[14] By carefully researching the motives, needs, preferences, and practices of their prospects before designing sales messages and selecting advertising media, advertisers and their advertising agencies are in

---

[13] Donald F. Cox, *Information and Uncertainty: Their Effects on Consumers' Product Evaluations,* 1962.

[14] Raymond A. Bauer, "Communication as a Transaction," 1963.

effect treating sales communication as a process. First they
learn about the audiences and then they develop communications and media designed to reach and persuade them. Bauer
argues, in effect, that as of 1963 formal academic studies in
communications phenomena have not generally been as aware
of this two-way transactional process as its commercial practitioners. Thus he says:

> The study of communications has traditionally (though
> not exclusively) been conducted from the point of view of
> *the effects intended by the communicator.* Viewed from this
> perspective, the disparity between actual and intended re-
> sults has often been puzzling. The key to this puzzle has come
> increasingly to be seen in entering the phenomenal world of
> the audience and studying the functions which communica-
> tions serve for him. The big failure in communications
> research to this point has been that the audience has not been
> given full status in the exchange relationship; his intentions
> have not been given the same attention as the intentions of
> the communicator.[15]

This call for viewing communications as a transaction in
which the audience plays a more powerful role than has cus-
tomarily been assumed provided a clear focus for a viewpoint
that had been somewhat more casually suggested in the preceding years by others. Thus in their 1953 review of research findings, Hovland, Janis, and Kelley in effect suggested that communications effects are not independent of audience "initiative"
when they called for research which isolated the effects of respondents' abilities and motives.[16] And in 1960 Klopper
published a book in which he summarized his position as "in es-
sence a shift away from the tendency to regard mass communication as a necessary and sufficient cause of audience effects,

---

[15] *Ibid.*
[16] *Op. cit.,* p. 289.

toward a view of the media as influences, working amid other influences, in a total situation." [17]

What are all of these "other influences" and what enters into the "total situation"? Rarick, for example, suggests that an important element in communications effectiveness, and one which has a bearing on the relative strength of the source effect, is the interest and emotional content of the message.[18] He concluded that, "The more interesting and novel the content, the less likely that the same degree of effective response to the source will distract the subject's attention from the content." [19] This implies that there is such a phenomenon as "message effect"—something about the message itself which has an influence independent of its source. But it suggests more. All other things being equal, message content can be "interesting" because of the subject of the message, because of the particular way the subject is treated or presented, or because of who is presenting it—who the communicator is, rather than necessarily the source of the message. Thus in addition to the "message effect" there may be a "presentation effect" (how it is presented) and a "communicator effect" (who presents it). And in all these cases, the "effect" is not something which the source or the communicator alone controls, but is in part "controlled" by the audience. It is "controlled" by the audience in the sense that the communicator organizes and presents his message in ways that are the result of assumptions he makes about what the audience values, how it thinks, and how it acts. What this in turn suggests is that there is indeed an "audience effect" and that it may vary from audience to audience, based on the Hovland, Janis, and Kelley distinction about differences between audiences' "abilities and motives."

---

[17] Joseph Klopper, *The Effect of Mass Communication,* 1960.

[18] Galen R. Rarick, "Effects of Two Components of Communicator Prestige," 1963.

[19] Summarized by Murray Hilibrand, *Source Credibility and the Persuasive Process,* 1964.

There are no published studies which make these clear-cut distinctions between source effect and audience effect, between message effect and audience effect, between message effect and presentation effect, between source effect and communicator effect. The latter distinction, if it is actually warranted, could be one of the most important in all communications phenomena. The reasons for this are that (1) experimental research, in its heavy preoccupation with source effect, has always implied or at least has always assumed that the communicator is also the source; and (2) in the real world of mass communications the communicator is very seldom the source. In commercial communications in particular the two are rarely identical. In television advertising, for example, the announcers and the bit players who speak in support of a product are the "communicators," but they are obviously not the "sources" of the messages they utter. The "sources" are the companies which produce and/or sell the products. The same distinction applies to the salesman's relationship to his employer and to the sales prospect to which he is speaking. In Bauer's language of the communications "transaction," a question therefore arises as to whether the usual focus in communications literature on source effect and on sleeper effect is really sufficient for understanding these elements of communications.

COMMUNICATIONS IN SELLING

In recent years business firms and advisors to business have shown increasing interest in the results of formal communications studies. Hence it is particularly useful to examine these studies in the light of the realities of the business community. In that community, not only is the communicator of a mass-communications message seldom the source of that message, but a variety of intruding variables are introduced into the communications process which have seldom been included in the experiments on which published studies are based. For example, most experiments in this area have involved exposing similar audiences to identical messages from different "sources." Hence differences in audience responses measure the differential effects of the sources on these audiences. Yet in commercial communications particularly, no two sources (companies) selling the same product to the same audience (customers) are ever likely to employ the identical message. Competing aspirin companies use different sales messages, as do competing manufacturers of identical bed sheets and competing manufacturers of polypropylene resin. Hence while it may be helpful to know that differences in the reputations (credibility) of competing companies can affect their sales effectiveness, this leaves many unanswered questions. Not only would one be interested in the relative importance of source effect and of communicator effect, but also in the relative importance of "message effect" within the context of source and communicator effect. That is, how do the character and the quality of the sales message itself modify what is known or knowable about the power of other effects?

Finally, there is the specific question of the character of audience initiative. Cox's finding [20] that an audience's level of generalized self-confidence affects its responses to sales messages suggests that an audience's level of competence to evaluate a message will also affect its responses or persuasibility. The question of such a possible "audience effect" is particularly important in commercial communications that are directed at audiences of varying degrees of responsibility for actions they may take in response to communications. Thus the recipient of a vendor's sales message may, for example, be either a novice or an expert on the subject of the message, or he may be in the position of a potential buyer of the vendor's product or merely a product evaluator who advises buyers. Hence the business community has a special interest in the question of the in-

---

[20] *Op. cit.*

fluence of the particular character and of the particular task of
the audience on its persuasibility. Except for the Bauer and
Cox studies (see footnotes 12 and 13), published communications research has not used "business" or "consumer" audiences
in its work. It has generally employed college students as subjects and it has not generally distinguished between differences
in audiences' competence and tasks.

The situation that therefore characterizes the use of mass
communications research findings in business is one in which:
(1) the results are based on experiments that have not, by and
large, employed commercial situations; (2) they have not generally employed commercial subjects of varying but known
degrees of competence; (3) they have not employed varying
messages or differences in message quality; (4) they have not
distinguished between differences in the tasks or responsibilities
of the subjects relative to the actions or opinions advocated by
the sources; and (5) they have not distinguished between the
source and the communicator in measuring source effect.

COMPANY REPUTATION IN INDUSTRIAL SELLING

The present monograph reports on research that, by focus-
ing on industrial seller-buyer relationships and studying the
matters listed in the foregoing paragraph, not only examines
some of the neglected aspects of communications phenomena
mentioned earlier; it also provides some possible guidelines
about the appropriate mix of industrial selling efforts. Since industrial selling almost always requires a face-to-face relationship between the seller or the seller's agent and the customer or
his agent, there is the question of the importance of this relationship relative to the prestige, reputation, or credibility of the
seller. That is, examination of industrial purchasing behavior
facilitates the determination of whether audiences distinguish
between a message source and a message transmitter. This is a
question of utmost importance to producers and sellers of in-

dustrial products. Yet it is a matter surrounded with ambiguity and confusion. For example, one author says that:

> In evaluating the salesman as a source of information about the value of a company as [an industrial products] supplier, one must recognize the strong impression that is left in the mind of the buyer by the character and personality of the salesman. Generally, the salesman is the only point of contact between the two companies, and the buyer tends to identify the company with its salesman. *If the salesman is reliable, cooperative, and competent, the buyer is inclined to assume that the company he represents is also reliable, cooperative, and competent.*[21]

But this picture of the source of a company's reputation is clouded by Shoaf's study of emotional factors in industrial purchasing which advises salesmen that, "The buyer sees you as a personification of your company and reflects its corporate image in the way you dress, act, and talk. Be honest, reliable and friendly." [22] Hence the company is assumed to have an "image" which the salesman merely "reflects," but presumably his failure to reflect it "properly" will cause the image to change. The question of where the "image" comes from in the first place is suggested by this study as being, for the most part, company advertising. But specifically advertising of "the company," not primarily advertising of its products. Thus one interpreter of the Shoaf study declares, "As time goes on, the belief increases . . . that the importance of making the market aware of a company's reliability or capabilities or enterprise transcends that of promoting the product's characteristics." [23] This theme was most effectively publicized and is perhaps best remembered

---

[21] John H. Westing and Isidor V. Fine, *Industrial Purchasing,* 1961, p. 72. Italics added.

[22] F. Robert Shoaf, *Emotional Factors Underlying Industrial Purchases,* 1959, p. 63.

[23] Howard G. Sawyer, "How to Use Emotional Factors in Your Advertising to Metalworking," in Shoaf, *op. cit.,* p. 52.

by the famous McGraw-Hill advertisement of a stern-looking purchasing agent facing the reader from behind his desk and saying:

"I don't know who you are.
I don't know your company.
I don't know your company's product.
I don't know what your company stands for.
I don't know your company's customers.
I don't know your company's record.
I don't know your company's reputation.
Now—what was it you wanted to sell me?"

MORAL:
Sales start before *your salesman calls—with business publication advertising.*
[See Exhibit 1-1.]

In recent years there has been a great upsurge in "corporate image" advertising and "corporate identity" programs designed primarily to "sell the company" rather than its specific products. But England concludes that:

As a general source of information to purchasing officers, the exact value of industrial advertising is a matter of dispute. . . . In spite of much that has been said in support of this contention [that industrial advertising is of great value], there is some question as to whether such advertising is as good or as useful as is often claimed.[24]

England points out, as others have done, that such "advertising may be designed to influence the buyer either as to choice of product or as to the source from which he buys." [25] But he concludes from research by the National Association of Purchasing Agents that "it would appear that only about one-eighth of the purchasing agents consider advertising one of the im-

---

[24] Wilbur B. England, *Procurement: Principles and Cases*, 1962, p. 411.
[25] *Ibid.*, p. 411n.

portant influences upon the choice of vendors." [26] Westing and Fine agree that the direct influence of industrial advertisements may be weak but that, "If they condition the buyer to give a more ready welcome to the advertiser's salesman or if they remind the buyer to inquire about the advertising company's product before buying, they have served a profitable purpose." [27]

The exact extent to which such advertising is "profitable" has been a subject of only modest study. Studies have approached the problem in two ways: (1) from the viewpoint of how industrial buyers evaluate suppliers in general, and (2) from the viewpoint of advertising expenditures as a percentage of the seller's marketing mix. The National Association of Purchasing Agents, on the basis of its studies, has issued a publication on *Evaluation of Supplier Performance* (1963) which supplies three different rating systems to help guide buyers on vendor selection. Some of the rating points on each of these plans are based on strictly objective measures, such as the vendor's delivery performance and price levels. But others involve subjective measures of vendor "reliability" in which advertising claims could conceivably influence the number of points a buyer assigns to a vendor. A review of a variety of vendor evaluation plans being used by several companies indicates that each has some element of the same subjective basis for ratings.[28]

Attempts at creating more objective systems are represented by several operations research and quantitative advertising evaluation studies. The operations research efforts are generally along the lines of suggesting approaches rather than the actual implementation of such approaches. This is particularly true of published works by Magee.[29] Research by Vidale and

---

[26] *Ibid.*, p. 412.

[27] Westing and Fine, *op. cit.*, p. 75.

[28] Somerby Dowst, "How Purchasing Agents Are Rating You," 1964.

[29] John F. Magee, "Some Approaches to Measuring Marketing Results," 1957, and "Operations Research in Making Marketing Decisions," 1960.

Wolfe [30] and by Brown, Hulswit, and Kettelle [31] have gone only slightly further by using a modest amount of customer behavior data as a basis for suggesting decision models that employ qualitative measures. But in no case was there a sufficient availability of behavioral information to implement the models fully. Professor Webster has similarly developed a purchasing decision model, but he himself contends that at its present stage it is little more than routinely descriptive. [32]

A study by the McGraw-Hill business publications [33] sought to determine whether more advertising by industrial firms lowered sales expense. If it did, it would be presumed that such advertising was an effective substitute for or aid to direct face-to-face selling. The 893-company sample showed, according to the research report, a consistent trend of lower total sales expenses being associated with "higher advertisers." That is, the higher the proportion of sales expenses spent on advertising, the lower was the percentage of sales expense to sales. The average resulting reduction of sales expense, regardless of company size, was 21%, ranging from 15% for "equipment and supplies" marketers to 27% for "materials and ingredients" marketers. On the basis of this conclusion that "sales expense is a smaller part of sales where advertising is a larger part of sales expense," John W. DeWolf, vice president for research of an industrial advertising agency, developed a method for determining the appropriate advertising expenditure for sellers of industrial products. [34] Without attempting to determine how advertising affects industrial sales, DeWolf's method in-

30 M. L. Vidale and H. B. Wolfe, "An Operations Research Study of Sales Response to Advertising," 1957.

31 Arthur A. Brown, Frank T. Hulswit, and John D. Kettelle, "A Study of Sales Operations," 1956.

32 Frederick E. Webster, "Modeling the Industrial Buying Process," 1964.

33 *How Advertising Affects the Cost of Selling,* 1963.

34 John W. DeWolf, "A New Tool for Setting and Selling the Advertising Budget," 1963.

EXHIBIT 1-1

"I don't know who you are.

I don't know your company.

I don't know your company's product.

I don't know what your company stands for.

I don't know your company's customers.

I don't know your company's record.

I don't know your company's reputation.

Now—what was it you wanted to sell me?"

MORAL:

Sales *start* <u>*before*</u> *your salesman calls—with business publication advertising.*

Reprinted with the permission of

McGRAW-HILL PUBLISHING COMPANY, INC., 330 WEST 42nd STREET, NEW YORK 36, N. Y.

volves the creation of an advertising-to-sales-expense break-even chart based on the McGraw-Hill data.

But there has been no rush toward the use of this method. The reason is obvious enough—nobody is really satisfied that he knows enough about the process by which customers (audiences) are influenced to be willing to develop sales budgets strictly by formula. Moreover, DeWolf's method provides no indication of how large the total sales expense budget should be or what the mix should be beyond the advertising ratio. The critical undecided variable remains a determination of how audiences are influenced. Knowing this, it is conceivable that a resulting change in advertising content and media selection, and a change in the character of the direct selling effort, would substantially alter the McGraw-Hill results and therefore the DeWolf formula. Beyond that, there remains the question, which was not treated in the McGraw-Hill study, of the way in which the formula varies as between new products and mature products, highly technical products and commodities, as between whether the purchasing decision makers are purchasing agents or, for example, design engineers, and so on. Thus a study done for *Scientific American* [35] shows that while design and development engineers participated in 20% of the decisions involving purchasing materials, they participated in 30% of the decisions involving component parts. Purchasing agents participated in 51% of the decisions involving plant equipment and 67% of the decisions involving materials. Regarding the stage of the decision-making process at which various participants were active, purchasing agents helped set specifications in only 7% of the cases, evaluated materials offered by vendors in 44% of the cases, but decided on the supplier in 67% of the cases. By contrast, design and development engineers helped set specifications in 51% of the cases, evaluated materials in 43% of the cases, but decided on the supplier in only 20% of the cases.

---

[35] *How Industry Buys,* 1965.

The "average industrial company spends from 40 to 60 per cent of sales income for the materials and services it purchases from outside suppliers. . . ." [36] and "In most industrial firms the procurement function spends a larger percentage of the sales dollar than any other function." [37] With procurement (or purchasing) officials therefore occupying such important roles as customers in American industry, with so much selling effort directed at them, and with so much ambiguity surrounding the relative importance of advertising and the seller's reputation versus direct face-to-face communication, the way in which the communications process works in the selling-buying situation in which business firms are involved is an especially appropriate area of investigation. It suggests the importance of a study of how source and sleeper effect findings apply specifically to an important area of commercial intercourse. The presumption is that such a study will provide clues about the relative value of advertising versus direct selling as applied to such situations. Thus, it might help provide clues about the relationship between corporate advertising and direct selling, about the relative value of advertising in the marketing mix of industrial firms versus spending more money on training salesmen, about the role of the salesman in helping create a company's reputation, and about how all this varies as between audiences of varying competences and subjected to different degrees of risks in the purchasing decisions they are asked to make.

OBJECTIVES OF THE PRESENT STUDY

The present monograph reports on research designed to explore the questions and issues raised above. Specifically, the objectives of the research were:

---

[36] England, *op. cit.*, p. 1.
[37] *Ibid.*, p. v.

1. To determine how and to what extent source effect and sleeper effect, as conventionally defined, operate in communications between sellers and buyers of industrial products.
2. To determine whether and to what extent there is in such communications transactions a "message effect"—specifically, how the character and quality of the message impinge on source and sleeper effect.
3. To determine whether and to what extent there is in such communications transactions a "communicator effect"—specifically, whether and to what extent there is a difference between the effect of the source and the effect of the message transmitter.
4. To determine whether and to what extent there is in such communications transactions an "audience effect"—specifically, how the competence and the task of the audience impinge on communications effectiveness and how they impinge on source and sleeper effect.
5. To determine whether and to what extent in such communications transactions audience persuasibility is related to:
   a. How well the audience learns and retains factual information contained in the message.
   b. Self-confidence of the audience in its own reactions to the message.

Given the growing business interest in communications research, the study of these phenomena in the context of commercial affairs is particularly apropos. Although business firms and university teachers of business subjects are increasingly using the results of the kinds of communications research referred to above, the present author knows of only two pieces of such research that employed commercial situations or subjects—one by Cox (see footnote 13) and one by Bauer (see footnote 12). The first of these was not completed until 1962, and neither employed industrial product situations. On the other hand, while there have been a variety of published studies of advertising's role in the selling or buying of industrial products, none of these has employed the methods or sought to test the theories of communications researchers who have worked with other materials and subjects. The present research is designed in part to fill these gaps.

The findings reported in the following chapters are based on a research device which attempted to simulate some of the basic factors involved in the confrontation of an industrial materials salesman and his prospects. In addition, it attempted to simulate some of the pressures and conditions under which the prospects operate.

Hence the research is, in effect, a clinical experiment. But all experimental research suffers from the single great limitation of its being experimental. Its findings are generalizable only as far as the design of the research instrument approximates the conditions to which generalizations are directed. It is therefore important to describe the research mechanism in detail. This is done in Chapter 3, with a brief summary provided in the paragraphs that follow.

Basically, the research involved dividing three distinctly different audiences—currently employed industrial purchasing agents, currently employed technical personnel (which are referred to here, in short, as "chemists"), and full-time graduate students of business administration—into two groups each. Each of these audience groups was separately exposed to a single filmed salesman's presentation for a new, technically complex ingredient used in the manufacturing of paint. Hence there were six audience groups—two purchasing agent groups, two chemist groups, and two student groups. There were two different ten-minute filmed sales presentations for the same product, a "good" presentation and a "poor" presentation. The stages (or sets) of both films were identical, as were the actors and the roles they played. One purchasing agent group saw the "good" film and one saw the "poor" film. Similarly, one chemist group saw the "good" film and one saw the "poor" one. The same was done with the students. In short, each group of each of the various audiences was exposed to one film in the following manner:

AUDIENCES

Type of film seen	Group I			Group II		
	Purchasing Agents	Chemists	Students	Purchasing Agents	Chemists	Students
"Good"	x	x	x			
"Poor"				x	x	x

Immediately after each audience group saw its particular film, each viewer filled out two detailed questionnaires, and then a third follow-up questionnaire was filled out five weeks later.

Before seeing its film, and then again before executing its questionnaires, each audience was given detailed instructions regarding the vantage points from which to view its film and from which to fill out the questionnaires. Purchasing agents and students were both asked to assume they were purchasing agents for a paint manufacturer. Chemists were asked to assume they were chemists for a paint manufacturer. The character and responsibilities of the jobs they were asked to assume they held in the company that employed them were described at some length.

In addition to dividing each audience category (purchasing agents, technical personnel, and students) into two groups each—one to see the good sales presentation and one to see the poor presentation—the films which each of these six groups saw were distinctive for each exposure in one other respect. A third of each of the six groups had its salesman in the film identified as being from the Monsanto Chemical Company, which in the research is classified as a "high-credibility source." [38] Another third of each of the six groups had its salesman in the film identified as being from the Denver Chemical Company, a "medium-credibility source." And the remaining third of each of the six groups saw a filmed salesman from an anonymous

[38] At the time of the present research Monsanto's name had recently been changed to "Monsanto Company." Because of the greater familiarity of the previous name, it was used in the research with Monsanto's kind permission.

company ("low-credibility source"), in which the name of the
company was clearly blocked out in the film and in the film's
sound track.

Hence the "good" film was actually made up into three
"good" films, each of which was identical except for the fact
that in one the salesman was identified as being from "Monsanto," in one he was from "Denver," and in the third his company was anonymous. The "poor" film was made up into the
same three sets. As the result, the final exposures of the various audiences were as follows:

		AUDIENCES					
		Group I			Group II		
Types and salesman identification of films seen		*Pur- chasing Agents*	*Chem- ists*	*Stu- dents*	*Pur- chasing Agents*	*Chem- ists*	*Stu- dents*
"Good"	Monsanto	x	x	x			
	Denver	x	x	x			
	Anonymous	x	x	x			
"Poor"	Monsanto				x	x	x
	Denver				x	x	x
	Anonymous				x	x	x

The film scripts were pre-tested to assure that the credibility assumptions ("high" vs. "medium-to-low") and the film
quality assumptions ("good" vs. "poor") were properly justi-
fied. The possibility of information migration between the various audiences was carefully controlled by having each viewer
group within an audience category (purchasing agents, chemists, students) see its film in a different room at the same moment every other viewer group of that audience category saw
its film. Furthermore, each type of audience saw its set of films
in a different geographic location.

The viewers of the films were required to make several types
of responses in the questionnaires they answered:

a. Decisions as to whether they would recommend giving the proposed new ingredient a further hearing in their companies.
b. Decisions as to whether, if they had full authority to make decisions, they would adopt the new ingredient.
c. Ratings of their self-confidence in the decisions they made.
d. Ratings regarding the quality of the sales presentation, the reliability of the product and the vendor company, and the trustworthiness and the knowledgeability of the salesman.
e. Answering questions designed to determine how much of the film's factual information was retained.

* * * * *

Chapter 2 of the present monograph consists of a relatively brief summary statement of the major findings of the research. This statement deals primarily with the central thrust of the findings, including a modest statement of their importance to the business community. The final chapter of the monograph, Chapter 7, contains a more elaborate review of the findings, with detailed emphasis on their possible meaning for both the business community and communications researchers.

Chapter 3, as pointed out above, describes the research method in detail.

Chapter 4 is an analysis of source, presentation, audience, and sleeper effects, with special emphasis on the relation of these findings to the published findings of other communications research.

Chapter 5 examines the role of four variables in the respondent decision-making process: respondent self-confidence, respondent trust in the message source and in the message communicator, the riskiness of the decision the respondent was asked to make, and the amount of information retained by the respondent.

Chapter 6 reports in more detail on how source, presenta-

tion, and audience effects are related to respondents' evaluations of the salesman's filmed presentations and on their
evaluations of the salesman's familiarity with the customer's
problems.

In each of Chapters 4, 5, and 6 the findings are discussed
in terms of the two general categories of interest suggested
above—their relevance and significance for the psychological
and behavioral insights of communications research, and their
relevance and significance for the marketing practices of business firms selling industrial products. In the latter case, the
emphasis is on the relative importance of advertising versus
direct selling efforts and on the character of these efforts.

CHAPTER 2

Management Summary

THE MAJOR FINDING of this study is that for complex industrial products or materials a company's generalized reputation has an important bearing on how its sales prospects make buying decisions. Generally speaking, the better a company's reputation, the better are its chances (1) of getting a favorable first hearing for a new product among customer prospects, and (2) of getting early adoption of that product. But, although a good generalized reputation is always useful, it is more effective in obtaining a favorable first hearing for a new product than in obtaining its actual early adoption. In other words, the greater the risk the customer is asked to take (product adoption versus merely agreeing to give it a further and closer look), the less important seems to be the vendor's reputation in influencing the customer's decision.

The riskiness of the decision which the listener to a sales presentation is expected to make affects his susceptibility to what has been called "source effect"; i.e., the phenomenon of the reputation or credibility of the source of a message becoming a factor in the impact of that message on the audience to which it is directed. The greater the risk which audience acceptance of, or concurrence with, the message implies, the less is the audience's susceptibility to the power of the source's reputation. From the point of view of a producer of industrial materials or components, this means that the cultivation of a good reputation among potential customers will have some payoff in the sense that it will help his salesmen to get "a foot into the door" of a prospect. But the value of cultivating a good reputation seems to be considerably less when it comes to its effect on the likelihood of the prospect actually buying a new product upon being first exposed to it. A good reputation always helps, but it helps less as the riskiness of the customer's decision rises and he has something else to rely or draw on.

SOURCE, AUDIENCE, AND PRESENTATION EFFECTS

While these are the general over-all conclusions of the study whose results this monograph reports, there are a great many important variations within the broad sweep of the results on which these conclusions are based. The research found, for example, that the power of source effect (company reputation for credibility) varies by the character and "competence" of the recipient of a sales message. Thus there is some indication that, in the case of complex industrial materials, purchasing agents, who are usually highly competent as professional buyers, may be less influenced by a company's generalized reputation than technical personnel, who are presumably less competent as buyers but more competent as judges of a complex product's merits. In first appraising complex new materials on the basis of sales presentations made directly to them, technically sophisticated technical personnel seem to be influenced by the seller's reputation to a point that is unexpectedly higher than the influence of that reputation on such technically less sophisticated personnel as purchasing agents. In short, technical personnel are probably influenced far more by company reputation than has been widely assumed, and certainly more than such technically less sophisticated people as purchasing agents. This seems to suggest that a producer of technically advanced products which are used as components or as ingredients by other manufacturers would be wise systematically to cultivate for himself a strongly favorable generalized reputation among technical personnel of prospective manufacturing customers. In other words, in trying to sell such products to technically trained personnel it may not be wise to rely so unevenly on the product's inherent virtues and on making strong technical product presentations. Technical personnel are not human computers whose purchasing and product-specification decisions are based on cold calculations and devoid of less rigorously rational influences. They do indeed seem to be influenced by the seller's general reputation.

However, as might have been expected, the quality of a salesman's presentation in support of a product was found to be an important variable in obtaining favorable buyer (audience) reactions. Regardless of the technical or purchasing competence of the audience, a good direct sales presentation was generally more effective than a poor one. In other words, there was a "presentation effect" in favor of the product supported by a well-done sales presentation. But, as in the case of source effect, the research indicates that a good sales presentation is generally more useful in getting a favorable first hearing for a new product (i.e., in what is, for the audience, a low-risk decision) than it is in getting a favorable buying decision (i.e., a high-risk decision). A good sales presentation is definitely better than a poor one in getting product adoption, but it is even better than a poor one in getting a favorable first hearing for a product.

Combining the influences of source effect and presentation effect, the research suggests that when a relatively unknown or anonymous company makes a good direct sales presentation, this combination may be just as effective in getting a favorable first hearing for a complex new industrial material as the combination of a well-known company making a poor presentation. Thus a well-known company loses the advantage of its reputation if its direct sales presentation is clearly inferior to that of an unknown or little-known company. Against a good sales presentation by a little-known company, a well-known one must also have a good presentation if the customer-getting value of its reputation is to be realized. Conversely, a little-known company, by concentrating strongly on training its salesmen to make good presentations, may be able to make considerable progress toward overcoming the liability of its relative anonymity.

While the research suggests that all audiences seem to be influenced by the quality of the sales presentation (presentation effect), important differences apparently exist between purchasing agents and technical personnel. In the lower-risk decision situation of whether to give a newly presented complex new product a further hearing, technical personnel were more powerfully influenced by the quality of a direct sales presentation than were purchasing agents. Put differently, on low-risk purchasing decisions, the technically less sophisticated purchasing agents seem to have relied less heavily on the quality of the sales presentation than did the technically more sophisticated personnel in making their decisions. But on high-risk decisions (whether actually to buy the product) the reverse was true. That is, the greater the risk, the more favorably purchasing agents were influenced by good sales presentations, and the less favorably technical personnel were influenced by such presentations. The greater the risk, the more likely technical personnel were to rely on their technical judgments about a new product's virtues rather than on the quality of the sales presentation in favor of that product. But purchasing agents, being technically less sophisticated, seem forced, in high-risk situations, to rely more heavily on the seller's presentation.

All this indicates that both the reputation of a vendor company and the quality of its direct sales presentations are important elements in sales success, but that the way the importance of these elements varies as between audiences and between types of audience decision-situations greatly affects how a vendor might wish to shape his marketing tactics.

SLEEPER EFFECT AND ITS VARIABLES

The present research also suggests that "sleeper effect" works about as much in industrial sales situations as it does in other areas to which study has been directed. Thus the favorable influence of a company's generalized good reputation (source effect) was found to erode with the passage of time, as did the unfavorable influence of a company's ambiguous reputation or anonymity. In short, in the absence of repeated callbacks or advertisements to reinforce the identity of the source, a seller tends, over time, to lose the favorable impact of his good reputation on the attitudes and actions of his sales prospects. As time passes, the power of source effect on audience decisions declines.

Interestingly, however, there is some evidence that the more self-confidently a prospect refuses at the outset to permit a new product to be viewed and reviewed by others in his firm, the greater the likelihood later that he will change his mind and give such permission. That is, a strong outright refusal for a further hearing at the time of the first sales call may suggest greater probability of getting permission later for another hearing than does a weak and vascillating original refusal.

Generally speaking, the better the original sales presentation, the greater the durability of its influence on the audience with the passage of time. That is, regardless of the presence of sleeper effect (the declining influences of source credibility with the passage of time), if the original sales presentation was relatively good, the audience tended more strongly to favor the product in question at a later date than if that presentation was poor. In other words, the originally favorable influence of the highly credible source declined less, and the originally unfavorable influence of the less credible source hurt less, as the original sales presentation was better. A good sales presentation has greater durability than a good company reputation. Company reputation, in order to work for that company, has to be more regularly reinforced (possibly through advertising repetition) than does the effect of a good sales presentation.

Respondents' feelings about sources, messages, and salesmen

One feature of the research reported in the present monograph was that it not only attempted to measure the direction of people's responses to particular sales messages, but also the strengths of these responses and the repondents' attitudes toward and feelings about the sources of these messages. Thus, the research showed that in making low-risk decisions (such as referring the product onward to others in the company), respondents had about as much self-confidence in their positive as in their negative decisions. But in high-risk decisions (actually adopting or buying the product), respondents were much more self-confident on negative than on positive decisions.

This confirms the perfectly common-sense expectation that the greater the personal risk to the respondent (customer), the more persuasion it takes to get him to switch from an opinion he already holds or a product he is currently using. It also suggests that once an audience (customer) has made a decision in a high-risk situation, the communicator (seller) will generally have considerable difficulty both in getting the negative respondent subsequently to change his mind and in keeping the affirmative respondent from changing his mind. This means that, especially in high-risk situations, it pays to try to get a favorable customer decision at the outset. Once he has rejected a product, it appears to be extremely difficult to get the prospect to be willing to re-open the discussions. Similarly, once he has accepted a new product under high-risk conditions, the customer appears to suffer from considerable self-doubt about whether he has made the right decision. He is probably very susceptible to being "un-sold" by a competitor. This suggests the need for continuous follow-up by the original seller to re-assure the customer and thus keep him sold.

It has already been pointed out that, generally speaking, the more credible the source the more likely it is that its message will get a favorable reception. But the question arises of who "the" source is: Is it the salesman who makes the sales call, or is it the company he represents? Do audiences (customers) perceive these two "sources" as being the same or different? The present research indicates that they think of them as being two different sources. The salesman is not automatically thought of as being the company. Thus, when asked to rank the trustworthiness of the salesman on the one hand and then the trustworthiness of the company he represented, respond-ents consistently scored the salesman lower than his company.

While this probably reflects the relatively low esteem with which salesmen are generally held in our highly sales-depend-ent society, a closer look at the results suggests a great deal more. It was found, for example, that respondents were more likely to favor the products of salesmen whom they ranked low in trustworthiness when these salesmen represented well-known companies than they were to favor the products of salesmen whom they ranked relatively high in trustworthiness but who represented unknown companies. A similar result occurred in connection with respondents' feelings about how well informed and competent the salesmen from high-vs.-low credibility com-panies were. Thus offhand it would seem that favorably well-known companies operate at the distinct advantage of being able to afford to have less "trustworthy" and less "competent" salesmen, at least in the short run, than little-known or anony-mous companies. But close examination (in Chapter 5) sug-gests that this means that source effect is such a uniquely pow-erful force that for respondents to favor well-known companies their need to trust the salesmen of these companies and to think highly of their competence is much less urgent than it is in order for them to favor less well-known and anonymous companies. In other words, the favorably well-known company does indeed have an advantage over its less well-known competitor in that its salesmen need to seem less trustworthy and competent in order to be effective. Well-known companies need not be as scrupulous in their hiring and training of salesmen. Source effect seems almost to conquer everything.

But not entirely everything. As noted above, presentation quality and quality of the message can overcome some of the disadvantages of being relatively anonymous. So can, of course, trust in the salesman. What is it then that makes for an appearance of salesman trustworthiness? First of all, the results of the present research suggest that trustworthiness of the communicator (such as, for example, a salesman, television announcer, etc.) was not as clearly related to the audience's feelings about his knowledge or understanding of the product he was selling as might be expected. While there was some relationship, trust was much more closely related to the over-all quality or character of the salesman's sales presentation. Poor presentations particularly reduced trust in the message transmitter (salesman). They also reduced trust in the message source (the salesman's company). In other words, the better the presentation the more trustworthy both the company and the salesman were perceived to be. To say this, and what has been said before, is equivalent to saying that there may be considerable merit in making sure that salesmen have quality sales presentations, and this holds particularly for less well-known companies.

It is interesting to note from the research that there was only a very modest, certainly not a clear, connection between audience ratings of a salesman's trustworthiness and their judgments regarding the extent of his product competence. An audience's willingness either to recommend or adopt a product was not clearly related to its judgment about a salesman's product knowledge. Nor was it related, in the short run, to how much of the information which the salesman gave out that was actually retained by the audience.

All this suggests that in making its adoption decisions an audience (a customer) is influenced by more than what the salesman specifically says about the product or even how effectively he communicates product facts. It seems very probable that the communicator's personality and what he says about things other than the product in question play a vital role in influencing his audience. The effective transmission of product facts seems to be more important in the long run than in the immediately short run. With the passage of time since the date of the original sales presentation, persons who retained more product information right after that presentation were more likely to make and hold to decisions favorable to the source. Hence the importance of the effective transmission of product facts during the original presentation seems to increase as the product-adoption decision is delayed. But it is not clear that detailed recall of product facts ever becomes a paramount ingredient in obtaining favorable buying decisions.

In brief summary, it seems clear that company reputation is a powerful factor in the industrial purchasing process, but that its importance varies with the technical competence and sophistication of the customer. The quality of a sales message and the way it is presented are capable of moderating the influence of this "source effect," but again it varies by audience. Generally speaking, it pays for a company to be favorably well known, and perhaps especially among customers having some degree of technical sophistication, such as engineers and scientists. But superior sales messages and well-trained salesmen can help less well-known companies to overcome some of the disadvantages of their relative anonymity. A well-planned and well-executed direct sales presentation can be an especially strong competitive weapon for the less well-known company. Moreover, the greater the riskiness of the purchasing decision the customer is asked to make, the more likely is a good sales presentation to produce a customer decision in favor of the direction advocated by the source.

Summary of Findings, by Relative Value and Conclusiveness

THE FOLLOWING LISTING classifies the findings of importance to the business community in terms of both their relative usefulness and the degree of confidence one could have in the conclusiveness of the findings. This latter designation is the result of the fact that some of the research conclusions are more strongly supported by the research evidence than others. The conclusions may be divided according to the following grid.

Conclusiveness of Results

	High	*Medium*
Value of Results — *High*		
Low		

The following classification of conclusions uses this grid. In the headings employed below, the vertical-axis classification comes first and the horizontal-axis comes second. Thus "High-High" refers to "high" value and "high" conclusiveness; "High-Medium" refers to "high" value and "medium" conclusiveness.

HIGH-HIGH

1. When a company is generally well known, this fact helps its salesmen get a favorable first hearing for a new product and facilitates the prospect's early adoption of the product.
2. When the salesman from such a company also makes a good sales presentation, the result is both an improved likelihood of a favorable first hearing and greater likelihood of the product's early adoption by the prospect. Indeed, when it comes to obtaining direct adoption of a new product by a prospect, and assuming all vendors, regardless of their reputations, have the identical product, there is no substitute for a good sales presentation.
3. A good company reputation is less powerful in obtaining early customer adoption of a new product than it is in obtaining a favorable first hearing for that product. In short, as the riskiness of the action the customer is expected to take rises, the likelihood of the customer's being influenced by the seller's good reputation declines. Hence, the seller would be wise to take whatever actions he can to reassure the prospect and thus reduce his perception of the risk to which he exposes himself in making a decision favorable to the seller.
4. Regardless of the prospect's risks or the quality of a sales presentation, having a good reputation, or simply being well known in a not unfavorable way, is always better than being a less well-known or a completely anonymous company.
5. The effects of a company's reputation on the product-adoption decisions of a customer-prospect vary, not only by the riskiness of the decisions being made, but also by the in-company functions and "competencies" of the individuals making the decisions. Thus, purchasing agents are relatively less susceptible than technically trained personnel (such as chemists and engineers) to the influence of a company's good reputation. This is true regardless of whether they are asked merely to give the product a favorable first hearing or to make the relatively risky decision of actually adopting the product.
6. Purchasing agents are also less susceptible to the effects of a good sales presentation in a low-risk (first hearing) situation

than technical personnel, but more susceptible to such a presentation than technical personnel in a high-risk (adoption) situation. But a good direct sales presentation in all situations is better than a less-good presentation. Presentation, like company reputation, always makes some difference.

7. All this means that different sales prospects (even within the same firm) may have to be approached differently, and beyond that, they may each in turn have to be approached differently according to the riskiness of the decisions they are being asked to make.

8. When a relatively unknown or anonymous company makes a good direct sales presentation, this combination may be just as effective in getting a favorable first hearing for a complex new industrial material as the combination of a well-known company making a less-good presentation. A well-known company loses the advantage of its reputation if its direct sales presentation is clearly inferior to that of an unknown or little-known company. In short, a little-known company, by concentrating heavily on training its salesmen to make good sales presentations, may be able to make considerable progress toward overcoming the liability of its relative anonymity.

9. The favorable influence of a company's generalized good reputation erodes with the passage of time. In the absence of repeated salesmen's callbacks or advertisements to reinforce the identity of the vendor company, that company tends, over time, to lose the favorable impact of its good reputation on the attitudes and actions of its sales prospects.

10. The better a direct sales presentation, the greater the durability of its favorable influence over the prospect with the passage of time, regardless of the reputation of the seller or the in-company function or "competence" of the individual to whom the presentation is directed.

11. But the influence of a good sales presentation has greater effective durability than a company's non-reinforced favorable reputation.

12. In relatively low-risk purchasing decisions (for example, to give the product a further hearing), neither purchasing agents nor technical personnel exhibited much difference in the self-

confidence they had in their affirmative versus their negative responses. But in high-risk situations (product adoption) both groups were visibly more confident in their negative than in their affirmative reactions. In short, the more the personal risk, the more persuasion it seems to take to get the customer to switch from an existing product to a new one.

13. The amount of detailed product information from a sales presentation that is retained by the sales prospect has little bearing on whether the prospect reacts favorably or unfavorably toward the product in the short run. However, once the customer has made a decision, the more information he retained the less likely he is to change his decision.

High-Medium

1. The greater a sales prospect's original commitment in favor of a new product, the less likely he is to change his mind later.
2. The more self-confidently a sales prospect refuses at the outset to permit a new product to be viewed and reviewed by others in his firm, and the more completely he personally rejects the product, the greater the likelihood that he will later change his mind and reconsider the product.
3. But once, under high-risk (adoption) conditions, a prospect has made an ordinarily self-confident decision about a new product, whether it was an affirmative or a negative decision, the seller will generally have considerable difficulty both in getting the negative respondent subsequently to change his mind and in keeping the affirmative respondent *from* changing his mind. Since, therefore, it is particularly difficult to get a prospect who has refused to adopt a new product to reconsider his decision, it would seem particularly advisable to make the greatest effort to get a favorable decision at the outset. Second chances at the prospect have lower chances of success.
4. Similarly, once a prospect has accepted a new product under high-risk conditions, the customer appears to suffer from considerable self-doubt about whether he has made the right decision. This makes him susceptible to being "un-sold" by a competitor, and suggests the need for continuous follow-up by

the original seller to reassure the customer and thus keep him sold.

5. In making a product-adoption decision, a sales prospect is influenced by more than what the salesman specifically says about the product or even by how efficiently he communicates the product facts. The salesman's personality and what he says about things other than the product in question play a vital role in influencing a sales prospect.

6. The purchasing professionalism of purchasing agents may at times work in favor of the less well-known company, particularly if its salesman makes a less-good presentation under conditions where the purchasing agent is asked to make a high-risk adoption decision. Thus, a purchasing agent may selectively overlook some of the deficiencies of the less well-positioned vendor in order to increase the number and therefore the competition among vendors.

7. Purchasing agents appear to be harder to convince on the basis of a direct sales presentation than technically trained personnel that they should switch to a substitute technical product. But having been convinced, if the presentation was relatively poor they are particularly vulnerable to efforts to change their minds.

8. Prospects apparently respond slightly better, all other things remaining the same, to salesmen who seem more interested in the problems of their customers than salesmen who seem more interested in explaining the character of the product they are trying to sell.

LOW-MEDIUM

1. The power of a company's favorable reputation is so great that for sales prospects to favor well-known companies, their need to trust the salesmen of these companies and to think highly of their competence is less urgent than it is for them to favor less well-known or anonymous companies. In short, the favorably well-known company does not need to be as careful as other companies in hiring salesmen who clearly communicate trust and competence.

2. There is not much connection between a sales prospect's feel-

ings about a salesman's trustworthiness and his judgments regarding the extent of the salesman's knowledge and understanding of the product he is selling.

3. A prospect's willingness either to recommend or directly adopt a product is not clearly related to his judgment about the salesman's product knowledge or, in the short run, to how much of the actual product information that the salesman gave out was actually retained by the prospect.

4. A prospect's trust in a salesman is less a function of the prospect's feelings about the salesman's knowledge or understanding of the product he is selling than of the over-all quality or character of the salesman's sales presentation. A poor presentation particularly reduces trust in the salesman, and to some extent also in the company he represents. Trust in a less well-known company is particularly damaged by a less-good sales presentation.

5. Not only is the better-known vendor-company more likely to be favored by the customer than the less-known company, but it is also better insulated against counter persuasion once a customer has made a purchase decision in its behalf.

6. The quality of the sales presentation affects the amount of self-confidence a prospect has in his response to that presentation. The confidence-producing effect of a good presentation accelerates over time, as does the confidence-detracting effect of a less-good presentation. Hence while the passage of time works "against" the non-reinforced sales message of a well-known company, it works "for" a well-presented message, regardless of the company.

7. Customer prospects, whether highly sophisticated regarding the product in question or not, have higher competence expectations of the salesman of a well-known company than of a salesman of a less well-known company.

8. In order to respond favorably to a sales presentation, the prospect needs to have less trust in the salesman of a well-known company and does not need to feel that he is as competent as the salesman of a less well-known company.

9. Customer feelings about the quality of a sales presentation are a modest predictor of whether these customers will give the

product further consideration, but no predictor of whether they would immediately buy the product. All this is slightly more true of purchasing agents than of technically more sophisticated personnel.

Low-High

1. A good sales presentation *results* in the sales prospect having greater self-confidence in his affirmative response to such a sales presentation than he does in his affirmative response to a less-good presentation; but to respond negatively (rejecting the product) after hearing a good presentation, the respondent must *have* greater self-confidence in this response than when he responds negatively to a less-good presentation.

CHAPTER 3

Research Design and Statistical
Testing Techniques

THE MOST COMMON and difficult problem in communications research, as perhaps in all social science research, is that of isolating the effects of the many variables that impinge on a problem. While various ways of measuring results and testing their statistical significance help isolate the effects of individual variables under multi-varied conditions, the social scientist has never felt as confident or been as successful with his research efforts as, say, the chemist working in his laboratory.

In communications research, attempts have been made to approximate the controlled conditions of the chemist's laboratory by means of experimental research instruments. The usual method has been to expose selected groups of relatively homogenous subjects to specific communications under isolated conditions. Subjects have then been given questionnaires whose responses the researchers have then analyzed.

THE RESEARCH DESIGN

The present research has employed essentially the same method but with three major differences. Most of the experimental communications research on which the literature of the field is essentially built has employed collections of college students as subjects. In nearly all cases these were undergraduates whose participation was more or less compulsory. The students were handy to the researchers, and so they were used. Second, the messages to which these audiences were exposed have generally consisted of real or manufactured newspaper editorials, speeches, pictures, or organizational literature. These were given to the subjects in typed or printed form. Sometimes carefully prepared tape-recorded interviews were prepared for the subjects to listen to. The subject matter has usually been something of general interest and on which, frequently, the subjects were likely to have opinions. The research has generally sought to measure opinion change.

The present research is different in the following ways:

1. It employed three entirely disparate groups of male subjects, two of them being employed full-time in business in responsible positions, and the other being graduate students of business administration. All subjects were volunteers, although they did not know for what they were volunteering other than to "see a brief movie put on by the university."
2. The message used in the present research was a filmed version of a sales presentation for a hypothetical (but plausible-sounding) "new" industrial product.
3. The questionnaires measured not only subjects' opinion changes, but also their action (or decision) changes under various assumed conditions.

The purpose of the research was (1) to determine whether and to what extent some of the better-known results of communications research—specifically the concepts of source effect and sleeper effect—apply to industrial purchasing situations; (2) whether there is a difference in the extent of their application as between technically sophisticated industrial purchasers (such as chemists) and technically less sophisticated but critical purchasers (such as purchasing agents) and business school students, and whether therefore it is safe, as most students of the subject have done, to generalize to other populations the results of research on one population; and

(3) whether in industrial purchasing situations a subject's opinion change is a reliable predictor of his probable action change.

In order to achieve the above objectives of testing the applicability of certain communications research findings to realistic industrial purchasing situations, the research mechanism sought to simulate reality as much as possible. Thus, the "message" was about an entirely new chemical ingredient for use in paint manufacturing; the message was presented by an industrial salesman (on film); and the "audiences" included purchasing agents who were professionally employed as industrial purchasing agents and commercially employed technical personnel. Furthermore, since sales presentations vary in quality, to approximate reality even more, two sales presentations were filmed for the same product and delivered by the same "salesman." One was, on the basis of a specifically structured pretest, defined as being a relatively "good" sales presentation, and the other a relatively "poor" one. Each was shown separately to an equal number of subjects from each subject category. Both lasted ten minutes, and both used the subjective camera technique whereby each viewer of the film (audience) felt himself actually to be a character in the movie. Each film used the identical setting, consisting of an office in a business firm. The "salesman" in the movie came into the office addressing a hidden camera that in effect sat behind the desk of the man who was assumed to occupy the office. The salesman spoke to the camera as if it were the customer in such a way that the viewer of the film felt himself to be the office occupant and being directly addressed by the salesman in a more-or-less realistic setting. The "camera" occasionally interrupted the salesman's presentation with cryptic comments and questions, but largely it was the salesman who spoke and showed close-ups of data and test results pertaining to his product.

The product—called Silcaspence, a new anti-settling agent for paint—was reasonably technical in nature. It is unlikely that any paint manufacturer would have substituted it for his present anti-settling agents without the advice of, and perhaps further testing by, his own chemists.

Nearly all medium-to-large industrial firms have purchasing agents on their payrolls. These are professional buyers through whom all salesmen calling on the companies are generally forced to go. Purchasing agents vary considerably in the extent of their formal technical training. As a group, however, they are substantially less technically sophisticated than, say, chemists. In their capacities as product purchasers for their companies they generally have authority to buy, without consulting others in their company, only certain classifications of products and involving certain-sized bills. On very large-sized orders, and on highly technical products or substitutions for ingredients or parts presently used by their companies, the buying decisions are made by others. Purchasing agents often listen to a salesman's first presentation of his product to a company. In such a case it is the purchasing agent's job to decide whether to send the salesman to see technically more informed or more authoritative people in the firm, or whether to tell him outright that his company is not interested.

The purchasing agent is expected to do a certain amount of screening to keep others in the company from being overburdened by salesmen making calls. A purchasing agent who is too strict in his screening may deny his company early access to important new developments. One who is too loose burdens others in the company too much and therefore risks reprimand. Beyond that, his pride in being the designated company agency to sift the good from the bad tends to induce him to do an intelligent screening job.

The audio portion of the script of each film—the "good" script and the "poor" script—was recorded on tape and pretested with four groups of eleven purchasing agents each to determine whether and by how much the scripts were actually perceived as being "good" and "poor." The results indicated that the audiences clearly discriminated between the two scripts, but not so much that the "poor" one was a lopsided strawman that was acceptable to nobody. It is reasonable to say on the basis of the pre-test that the two messages were perceived as being either "generally good" or "generally not so good." For purposes of simplicity, they are referred to in this monograph as either "good" or "poor."

The actual data about the product, the arguments for its use, and the laboratory and in-use tests to which the product was subjected—all these pieces of information appeared in both the good and the poor film. But in the poor film the salesman hurried through certain technical sections of the presentation too fast, and he hesitated and indicated annoyance at several points at which the good-presentation salesman was smooth and self-possessed. The good presentation was also distinguished by the salesman referring more frequently to his "customer" by name, by indicating greater familiarity with the customer's manufacturing facilities, and by complimenting the customer for certain of his achievements.

In addition to the films varying by the quality of the sales presentation, they varied by the company the salesman was said to represent. Thus, the "good" film actually consisted of one version in which, at two points in the film (near the beginning and near the end), the salesman identified himself as being from the "Monsanto Chemical Company," another in which he identified himself as being from the "Denver Chemical Company," and a third in which his company was not identified. Although this third version did not identify the company, it was made clear to the audience that this was no oversight. The clear intention was that the salesman's company should remain anonymous. Hence, when the salesman mentioned his company in the film, the sound track was cut out; and when he showed his calling card, the name was blocked out. While the names of the companies were therefore different in each of these three "good" films, the three films were in every other respect identical. Indeed, the three films were printed from a single master negative, the name changes being made by splicing in a few feet of different film at the appropriate places. The "poor" film was divided into three separate prints in the same way as the "good" one, and as a result, there were six separate films.

At a convention of the New England Purchasing Agents Association, representing a wide spectrum of industries, volunteers who did not know what they were volunteering for were randomly divided into six groups. Eighty per cent of the convention attendees participated in the experiment. All six groups simultaneously went into different rooms where each saw one of the six film versions. The lead footage of each film consisted of an identical narration telling each group it was about to see a film in which each audience member was to consider himself a purchasing agent for a paint manufacturer. The narration also asked the listener to make certain assumptions about his role in his company and how his company made product decisions. Appendix 3-A (page 55) contains the "poor" presentation script of the movie that was shown, including the script of the lead footage in which the narrator spoke.

Immediately after the movie, respondents were given Part I of a questionnaire, which identified the respondents by a code number. (See Appendix 3-B, page 63.) They were not told that there would be a Part II. Part I consisted of opinion, evaluation, and action questions. When all respondents had completed this questionnaire, they were asked to put it away and were given Part II. (See Appendix 3-C, page 66.) This consisted of information questions—questions designed to test how much of the technical information in the movie was retained by the audience. This questionnaire was given separately and after Part I so that respondents would not, upon discovering they had retained little information, permit this fact to influence their opinions, evaluations, and actions in Part I. Five weeks after showing of the film, each respondent received a follow-up questionnaire (Part III) at his place of employment. (See Appendix 3-D, page 68.) [1]

Six groups of volunteer graduate business school students saw the same films seen by the purchasing agents and were asked to make the same assumptions. As with the purchasing agents, each group saw its respective film at the identical hour as every other group. There was no information leakage between groups.

Finally, the six films were shown under identical conditions to six groups of volunteer technical employees in the Boston area. For purposes of simplicity they are referred to in this discussion as "chemists," but not all were chemists. All were college graduates in some field of engineering or science. The films were the exact same films seen by the purchasing agents and students, except that the introductory narration asked the viewers to assume they were chemists in a paint company. (The assumptions chemists were asked to make in both the narration and in the questionnaires are found in Appendix 3-D. Just as there were slight differences between the assumptions purchasing agents were asked to make and those which "chemists" were asked to make—strictly because they performed different functions—so there were slight differences in the phrasings of a few of the questions they were asked to answer.)

Exhibit 3-1 shows the number of subjects in each group who saw each movie. Thus, there was a total of 374 subjects; 130 saw a Monsanto film, 125 a Denver, and 119 an Anonymous film. Of the total viewers, 113 were purchasing agents, 130 were chemists, and 131 were students.

The selection of the three company "names" (Monsanto,

---

[1] It will be noted in Appendix 3-D that the "assumptions" in this questionnaire are geared to chemists, not purchasing agents. This is done only for presentation purposes in this discussion of the research instrument so as to show what the chemists were told. In the actual research, purchasing agents received a follow-up questionnaire containing their own assumptions.

EXHIBIT 3-1

RESEARCH DESIGN: Number of Subjects, by Type of Presentation,
Company Source, and Audience

Audience	Good Presentation			Poor Presentation			Total		
	Monsanto	Denver	Anon.	Monsanto	Denver	Anon.	Monsanto	Denver	Anon.	Total
Purchasing Agents	23	21	16	17	19	17	40	40	33	113
Chemists	25	20	22	21	20	22	46	40	44	130
Students	24	24	21	20	21	23	44	45	42	131
Total	72	65	59	58	60	62	130	125	119	374

Denver, Anonymous) to identify the companies the salesmen represented was designed to test source-effect influences. Monsanto is a well-known, highly respected, large American chemical company. It is not as well-known as, say, DuPont, and for purposes of the present research this was a distinct virtue. DuPont is so well and favorably known that there is a danger that most other companies suffer badly in comparisons. Therefore the use of a name of a favorably well-known company whose reputation is close to that of most well-known large chemical companies is ideal from the viewpoint of simulating realistic market conditions. Monsanto fits this requirement better than DuPont.

The "Denver Chemical Company" does not exist. But it has a plausible sound. The pre-test indicated that a good number of respondents thought it was an existing company, though they ranked its reputation below that of Monsanto. Thus, Monsanto can be described as a "high-credibility source" and Denver as a "medium-credibility source." That is, Monsanto has a very favorable, high-trust reputation; Denver has little reputation and is trusted somewhat less—certainly not distrusted or absolutely doubted. The anonymous company is, to the audience, an enigma. It has qualities of being a neutral source, a low-credibility source, and perhaps even a high-credibility source. The possibility of its being a high-credibility source in the minds of some respondents is suggested by the possibility that they might have believed that a purposely unidentified company was such a well-known company that its name *had* to be blocked out in order to avoid biasing the audience. How it was actually perceived is shown in the analyses in Chapters 4, 5, and 6.

The rankings of credibility ratings of the company names used in this study assumes that the level of credibility adhering to any one company was not associated with the quality of that company's presentation in the film or with the respondents' past experiences with one of these companies. Thus, the relatively high-credibility ratings of Monsanto, which is the only one the respondents could have had any experience with, is assumed to be based not on any such experience, but on the general reputation Monsanto has built up over the years through advertising, public relations, and general news. This assumption seems valid since it is unlikely that more than a very tiny fraction of the respondents were likely in their work to have had actual dealings with Monsanto or its products.

Aside from this research instrument's attempt to approximate a more realistic communications and business situation than most other researches in this area have thus far achieved, the present research design was also unique in its examination of the role of the quality of a message and the quality of its transmission in communications effectiveness. Thus, it not only used two different scripts to say the same thing, but the communicator (the actor who assumed the salesman's role and played out the scripts) also did qualitatively different jobs with each script.

As a result it is possible to examine, not only source effect, but also message effect and presentation effect, and how these interact and vary as between audiences (audience effect). It is possible to see, for example, whether source effect seems to be more powerful in particular situations than presentation effect—whether it seems better for an industrial products company to build a strong reputation via advertising, for example, or whether it seems better for it to select and train its salesmen better. Moreover, it is possible to see the extent to which, in one instance at least, one may or may not generalize to the entire population on the basis of experimental results with students.

STATISTICAL TESTING TECHNIQUES

There are a variety of tests with which one can examine the statistical significance of his research results.

Chapters 4, 5, and 6 of the present study present all the research results in the form of the mean scores or percentages of types of responses. This permits the application of a simple and legitimate test of statistical significance. The following table is an example of the format in which the results of the present study are presented in subsequent chapters of this monograph. The numbers in this table represent, for illustrative purposes, the percentage of affirmative answers in each cell to a particular question.

Audience	Monsanto	Denver	Anonymous
Purchasing Agents	60	70	50
Chemists	50	60	60
Students	40	60	40

This format permits comparing the results for each source (Monsanto, Denver, Anonymous) by each audience (purchasing agents, chemists, students) and the comparison of one audience's results with each other audience's results. For example, in the above hypothetical table we can ask the question of how well purchasing agents scored relative to chemists and students. Purchasing agents have three scores—60% affirmative respondents for those who saw a film with a salesman from Monsanto, 70% for those whose salesman was from Denver, and 50% for those whose salesman was from the Anonymous company. For each source, purchasing agents can be compared to each audience. In the case of Monsanto, the purchasing agents' affirmative response ratio of 60% is higher than the chemists' ratio of 50% and the students' ratio of 40%. Thus, in two out of two comparisons (purchasing agents vs. chemists and purchasing agents vs. students), purchasing agents had a higher per cent of positive responses. In the above table, purchasing agent responses can be compared with the other two audiences in six ways—two for Monsanto, as was just demonstrated, two for Denver, and two for Anonymous. The results show that in five out of a possible six comparisons the purchasing agents' affirmative ratios are higher. Binomial probabilities may be used to assess the statistical significance of such results.[2] In the present case such tests can be used to assess the strength of the evidence indicating differences among sources or audiences.

If there is no real difference in the mean affirmative ratio of purchasing agents and chemists, the probability that the sample mean ratio for purchasing agents would be greater than the sample mean for chemists is $1/2$. Similarly, the probability that purchasing agents in the study would have higher ratios on the average than students would, under the hypothesis of no difference, also be equal to $1/2$. In all there are six possible comparisons of purchasing agents with other groups (students and chemists). In each, under the hypothesis, the likelihood of a higher average ratio is $1/2$.

Our experimental results show that in five of the six comparisons the purchasing agents had higher average ratios of positive responses. The binomial probability of five or more comparisons out of six showing higher ratios if the probability of a higher ratio is $1/2$ turns out to be .109. Thus, if the three groups had identical population means, the likelihood that one would find purchasing agents with higher sample averages in at least five of the six cases is slightly greater than 10%. These results are therefore said to be significant at the 10% level. The evidence that purchasing agents have higher average ratios of positive responses than the other audiences is therefore strongly suggestive, and one may say that purchasing agents have higher positive response ratios at the 10% level of statistical signif-

---

[2] See Robert Schlaifer, *Introduction to Statistics for Business Decisions,* 1961, pp. 136–148.

icance. In short, the observed results are not due to chance but to a real difference in the ratios.

The binomial test is, generally speaking, a conservative test. It does not, for example, give extra weight, as does the Chi square test, for the magnitude of differences between figures that are being compared. Nor does it give extra weight for larger numbers of cases in any particular cell or subgroup. Hence the fact that certain comparisons in the present study (see, for example, Exhibit 4-3) seemingly attribute as much significance to a difference between 96% and 95% as they attribute to a difference between 96% and 69% cannot be suspect any more than the fact that the level of significance the Chi square test would have provided would, in effect, have weighted the two differences and to this extent "expanded" the amount of difference between 96% and 95%. Furthermore, if a difference is as between 96% and 95%, its more-or-less common-sense significance should probably be based, not on the assertion that "they are nearly identical," but on a consideration of how one would think about the results if they had been reversed—that is, instead of Group A saying "yes" 96% of the time versus Group B saying it 95% of the time, B would have said it 96% and A, 95%. Such a switch would presumably have more meaning than the assertion that 96% and 95% are really identical. The fact is that both numbers are not, say, 95%. One group's results are higher than another, and to treat them as being identical in this case is to say that the group with the higher figure might just as easily have the lower figure. Speaking probabilistically, this could be quite true. But the binomial test as used in the present study generally compares a good many more than just two numbers.

Thus, even if the absolute differences between groups of data are not of great magnitude, if systematic change or direction is apparent for a substantial group of cases, what counts is the incidence of that change or the frequency with which it occurs—that is, the overwhelming direction of the results, not their magnitudes. Hence in the subsequent chapters it will be seen that even though differences between the results in some of the compared cells may be small (say, 96% vs. 95%, or 7.1 rating points vs. 6.9), it is rare that the analysis draws any conclusion unless a substantial proportion of the compared cells move in the same direction (that is, say, in 9 out of 12 cells Group A rates higher than Group B) so that according to the binomial test the probability of this being chance is reduced to, say, about 20% or less.

The fact that any given cell may have a different numerical base and represent an entirely different group of respondents than another with which it is being compared does not alter the meaningfulness of the results. The binomial test and the measures of significance it yields have a built-in stringency based entirely on the proportion of compared cells that dominates, given any number of total cells.

Sales Presentation Script:
"Poor" Presentation Script, with Narration and "Assumptions" to Purchasing Agents and Students

1. (Narration, MOU: Narrator
   standing in set, front of desk.)

> NARRATOR (*reading from script, facing camera*)

In a moment you will see a brief movie. It will show a sales engineer making a presentation to you for a new product exactly as you would see him sitting across a desk. Pretend he is talking directly to you. You don't know him—have never seen or dealt with him before. After the movie is over, will you please open your envelope and complete the enclosed questionnaire. Please answer *all* the questions. When finished, insert the questionnaire into the envelope and hand it to the man on your way out of the room.

You will note that your questionnaire has a number in the upper right-hand corner. This is for coding purposes only. While we have your names and addresses in the envelopes, they will not be used in any way by us except to know to whom to mail a brief follow-up questionnaire later.

Now, about the movie. As we noted, it is a sales presentation for a new product. Pretend you are a purchasing agent of a manufacturer of a wide line of paints that you sell to other manufacturers and to retail paint and hardware stores. The product which the sales engineer in the movie will present to you is a relatively new product that is actually now on the market. This is something you need not pretend about. The product is actually on the market today, and it is relatively new. But pretend this is the first time which your company, and you as purchasing agent, have ever been presented with the product. Our purpose in the questionnaire you will fill out after the movie is to measure your reactions to the sales presentation in the movie.

1. Assume you are one of a half-dozen purchasing agents in a company manufacturing paint sold to industrial firms and to retail hardware and paint stores.
2. The product—Silcaspense, an antisettling agent—which the sales engineer in the movie offered to you is a relatively new product which is actually on the market.
3. Assume that the presentation made to you in the movie is the first time that Silcaspense was offered to your company, and that you had never before met this sales engineer.
4. Assume that your company has a group of chemists who evaluate new ingredients for your company's paint. They make the *final* decisions as to whether these ingredients are to replace presently used ingredients.
5. Assume that all sales engineers who call on your company must first go to the Purchasing Department where their presentations are heard and screened. The Purchasing Agent who hears the presentation has *full* authority to decide by himself whether to send a sales engineer on to a chemist in the company. You are the only Purchasing Agent in your company who heard the presentation you heard today.

Now, on with the movie.

FADE OUT:

FADE IN:

2. (MOU: Walters standing
shakes hands.)

WALTERS (*handing card*)

My name is Walters, and I'm with the Monsanto Chemical Company, and I want to tell you about a product that we're sure is great and right for your company.

3. (ECU: Card)

JONES

Good. Won't you sit down?

4. (CU)

WALTERS (*sitting*)

Thanks. We've been working for the last three years on paint settling problems. We've spent an enormous amount of time and money on this project. In fact, we set up an entirely separate lab. You see . . . .

FADE OUT:

FADE IN:

5. (MCU)

WALTERS

As I was saying, it's been a long haul, but now we've developed what we call Silcaspense, and we think it has a great future. It's really unique because it can be added to almost any paint by simple low-speed mixing. It can even be used in systems that don't use pigment grinding because it dispenses so easy. Once it's in the paint, it keeps the pigment from settling as well as any present antisettling agents.

6. (MS)

WALTERS (*business*)

Suspending agents now used by the paint industry either have to be ground into the paste or a separate pre-gel is formed with high shear equipment. Both are extra production steps. And with the pre-gel method, often it isn't stable so that there can be a lot of wastage and even reduced paint quality. Silcaspense saves extra production steps because it can be put *directly* into the paint dispersion pastes, and it cuts out the unstable and quality-cutting pre-gel stage.

7. (CU)

WALTERS (*leaning forward*)

This is what we've been working on all these years. This is the fruit of our tremendous labors, and it is this that everybody is so tremendously excited about. It has an enormous potential. We're sure of that.

(TILT DOWN TO ECU: JONES'
HANDS, NOTE PAD)

JONES

Well, that all sounds swell, but I don't think things are quite that simple. Putting your stuff directly into the paint can lead to problems—that's why these agents are now ground or mixed into a pre-gel.

8. (MCU)

WALTERS

Oh, well, that's precisely the point, don't you see? Silcaspense flows more smoothly in today's high-speed mixing equipment. A suspending agent with hard agglomerates requires the use of high energy grinding equipment. This is expensive and can also lead to expensive repair and maintenance costs. Because Silcaspense has soft agglomerates, it also cuts power costs. And it's cheap to use.

(TILT DOWN TO CU: JONES'
TWO FINGERS)

JONES (*two fingers*)

But we have two different plants. We use the grinding process in one and the pre-gel in another. Won't that mean that we'll have different cost problems in switching to your stuff?

9. (MS)

WALTERS

Well, if you use two different processes now this means you can standardize by using Silcaspense. There's no problem in switching. It's quite easy.

JONES

What are the economics?

WALTERS (*removes paper from briefcase*)

Here's a cost comparison with other suspending agents.

(*Walters stands. Places paper on desk.*)

EXHIBIT A-1

RAW MATERIAL COST ANALYSIS

Alkyd Flat Formulation

Material	Pounds Per 100 Gallons			Suspending Agent Cost Per Lb.
	#1	#2	#3	
Titanium Dioxide	235.0	235.0	235.0	
Calcium Carbonate	350.0	350.0	350.0	
Barytes	200.0	200.0	200.0	
Alkyd Resin (50% N.V.Z_2-Z_5)	300.0	300.0	300.0	
Mineral Spirits	184.0	184.0	184.0	
24% Lead Drier	2.0	2.0	2.0	
6% Cobalt Drier	1.1	1.1	1.1	
Antioxidant	0.85	0.85	0.85	
Antiflooding Agent	0.1	0.1	0.1	
Suspending Agents				
Silcaspense	4.0	—	—	70c
Suspending Agent #1	—	4.66	—	60c
Suspending Agent #2	—	—	7.0	40c
Total Gals.	100.0	100.0	100.0	
Suspending Agent Cost Per Formulation	2.8c	2.8c	2.8c	
	per gal.	per gal.	per gal.	
Total R.M.C. Per Gallon	$1.30	$1.30	$1.30	

Degree of Settling

Time	Silcaspense	Suspending Agent #1	Suspending Agent #2
1 Week	None	None	None
1 Month	None	None	None
6 Months	Very Sl. Soft Sediment	Very Sl. Soft Sediment	Very Sl. Soft Sediment
1 Year	Very Sl. Soft Sediment	Very Sl. Soft Sediment	Very Sl. Soft Sediment

10. (ECU: COST PAPER LANDS ON
    DESK.)

WALTERS (*voice over*)

What we've got here is the formula for an alkyd flat paint, except that the #1 formula contains Silcaspense and the #2 and #3 formulas contain other suspending agents. Ours (*pointing*) costs 70¢ a pound, and theirs costs either 60¢ or 40¢. But you need less of ours (*pointing to 4.0, 4.66, and 7.0*) so that in the end the cost of the suspending agent per gallon of paint is the same (*pointing to 2.8¢*) for all three formulas.

And, as you can see (*pointing fast to the bottom panel*), the settling characteristics of the three agents are identical. So—the costs per gallon of suspension are the same, even though Silcaspense costs more per pound. But since it cuts manufacturing costs, it's really cheaper.

11. (MCU)

WALTERS (*standing*)

And it can cut the usual rate of pigment fading too because of the way it raises paint viscosity. (*Sits down*) Also, Silcaspense is extremely fine—15 to 20 millimicrons. Coarse suspending agents that have a particle size of one-half to one micron produce large-size agglomerates that are more difficult to separate and require high energy grinding equipment which, in the end, adds up to high production cost.

(TILT TO ECU COST PAPER
ON DESK)

JONES

Well, maybe an awful lot of things are involved. Besides, I've seen a lot of these laboratory comparisons; and when it comes to actual production runs, the lab figures turn out to be way off base.

12. (CU: WALTERS' FACE. TILT
    TO BRIEFCASE)

WALTERS (*rummages in briefcase*)

Just a minute. I've got the answer to that one. I knew it was here somewhere. Just take a look at this. Here it is. (See Exhibit A-2.)

EXHIBIT A-2

PRODUCTION CASE HISTORIES

Size of Batch	Type of Paint	Dispersion Equipment	Date of Production
200 gallons	Red Lead Primer	3-Roll Mill	Sept. 3, 1962
200	Red Lead Primer	3-Roll Mill	Sept. 4, 1962
1000	Oil-Base House Paint	Stone Mill	Sept. 18, 1962
1000	Oil-Base House Paint	Stone Mill	Sept. 19, 1962
400	PVA Topcoat	High-Speed Mixer	Sept. 25, 1962
400	PVA Topcoat	High-Speed Mixer	Sept. 26, 1962
1000	Alkyd Flat	High-Speed Mixer	Oct. 15, 1962
500	Alkyd Flat	High-Speed Mixer	Oct. 16, 1962
250	Acrylic Emulsion	High-Speed Mixer	Oct. 20, 1962
250	Acrylic Emulsion	High-Speed Mixer	Oct. 21, 1962

(All paints were manufactured at reputable paint manufacturing plants which produced at least $2,000,000 gross annual sales. Names are available on request.)

SETTLING DATA ON ABOVE LISTED PRODUCTION BATCHES

Type of Paint	Suspending Agent	1 Week	3 Months	1 Year
Red	Silcaspense	None	None	Very Sl. Soft Sediment
Lead	Suspending Agent #1	None	None	Very Sl. Soft Sediment
Primer	Suspending Agent #2	None	None	Very Sl. Soft Sediment
Acrylic	Silcaspense	None	None	Very Sl. Soft Sediment
Emulsion	Suspending Agent #1	None	None	Very Sl. Soft Sediment
	Suspending Agent #2	None	None	Very Sl. Soft Sediment

13. (ECU: PAPER #2 LANDING
    ON DESK)

WALTERS (*voice over*)

These are the results of some actual production runs made with this material in five different plants using different dispersion equipment. We used a lot of different kinds of paints, and we tested in big reputable companies. As you can see (pointing vaguely to bottom half of the bulletin), these settling test results are precisely the same as we got in our lab tests. This proves that one of the unique qualities of Silcaspense is what I said earlier about how it can eliminate the grinding and pre-gel operation. All you need is that the mixer has to be run at a minimum of 400 RPMs.

14. (CU)

WALTERS (*seated*)

We've been working on this a long time, have spent a lot of time and money on it, and we know it works. We'd like to see you give it a try—maybe even evaluate it for yourself.

FADE OUT:

FADE IN:

15. (TITLE: A HALF HOUR
    DISCUSSION FOLLOWS)

DISSOLVE TO:

16. (MCU)

WALTERS (*rising, shakes hands*)

Thanks a lot for your time. I'll be back in about ten days. If you want any more information, you can reach me at Monsanto.

Questionnaire: Part I, with "Assumptions" to Purchasing Agents and Students

PLEASE READ CAREFULLY BEFORE ANSWERING QUESTIONNAIRE

Assumptions

1. Assume you are one of a half-dozen purchasing agents in a company manufacturing paint sold to industrial firms and to retail hardware and paint stores.
2. The product—Silcaspense, an antisettling agent—which the sales engineer in the movie offered to you is a relatively new product which is actually on the market.
3. Assume that the presentation made to you in the movie is the first time that Silcaspense was offered to your company, and that you had never before met this sales engineer.
4. Assume that your company has a group of chemists who evaluate new ingredients for your company's paint. They make the final decisions as to whether these ingredients are to replace presently used ingredients.
5. Assume that all sales engineers who call on your company must first go to the Purchasing Department where their presentations are heard and screened. The Purchasing Agent who hears the presentation has *full* authority to decide by himself whether to send a sales engineer on to a chemist in the company. You are the only Purchasing Agent in your company who heard the presentation you heard today.

QUESTIONS

1. You must now make a choice as to whether to send the sales engineer you heard today to see one of your company's chemists. Would you send him? (Please check one.)

    a. Yes _____

    b. No _____

2. How confident are you of the decision you made in answer to the above question? (Do *not* change the above answer.) On the following scale, place a check mark within the block which expresses the degree of confidence you have in your response to Question No. 1.

Very unconfident — Very confident

3. Given the product and its expected use, was the sales engineer's presentation (check one):
   a. Good _____
   b. Average _____
   c. Poor _____

4. Which of the following opinions do you *agree with most* (check one only):
   a. The product is better than the sales engineer implied _____.
   b. The product is about as good as the sales engineer implied _____.
   c. The product is not as good as the sales engineer implied _____.

5. Which of the following opinions do you agree with most (check one only):
   a. The quality of the sales presentation was better than the quality of the product itself _____.
   b. The quality of the sales presentation was about on par with the quality of the product itself _____.
   c. The quality of the sales presentation was worse than the quality of the product itself _____.

6. How well do you think the sales engineer knew the problems and operations of the company to which he was trying to sell? (Check one.)
   a. Very well _____
   b. Medium well _____
   c. Poorly _____

7. Suppose instead of sending the sales engineer on to a chemist, you personally had *full* responsibility in your company to

make the decision as to whether your company switches to the product the sales engineer offered. Would you switch?

    a. Yes _____

    b. No _____

8. How confident are you of your answer to question 7? (Check the block which expresses your feelings.)

Very unconfident |_|_|_|_|_|_|_| Very confident

9. We tend to have different feelings about the product claims made by various companies. Considering everything, what do you think about the product claims of the company the sales engineer represented—not just about the claims for this one particular product, but about the company's product claims generally? Please rank on the following scale your feelings about *this* company's over-all product claims.

Very unreliable |_|_|_|_|_|_|_| Very reliable

10. Salesmen vary in the degree of their knowledge of the products they sell. Please indicate your estimate of the salesman's knowledge of the product in the film you saw. (Please check one block.)

Very unknowledgeable |_|_|_|_|_|_|_| Very knowledgeable

11. When one listens to a sales presentation, one develops various degrees of trust in the salesman. How would you rate the trustworthiness of the salesman you saw in the film? (Please check one block.)

Very untrustworthy |_|_|_|_|_|_|_| Very trustworthy

    This ends the questionnaire. Please fold it and replace it in your envelope. Do *not* leave your chair yet.

Questionnaire: Part II

Please answer all the following questions:

1. The selling price of Silcaspense is the same as the products with which it competes. (Please check one.)
    True _____
    False _____
2. Silcaspense is designed to substantially reduce present paint settling problems.
    True _____
    False _____
3. Production-run tests verified Silcaspense laboratory tests.
    True _____
    False _____
4. On a per-gallon basis, tests showed that the cost of Silcaspense to the paint manufacturer would be (please check one):
    1.3¢ _____
    1.8¢ _____
    2.3¢ _____
    2.8¢ _____
    3.3¢ _____
    3.8¢ _____
5. In the laboratory tests of Settling Agent #1, very slow soft sediment showed up in (please check one):
    1 month _____
    4 months _____
    5 months _____
    1 year _____
6. When the suspending agent is ground into the paste during the paint manufacturing process, there is a danger of producing

an unstable formulation, with resulting waste and quality reduction.

     True _____

     False _____

7. One of the great advantages of Silcaspense is its relatively hard
agglomerates.

     True _____

     False _____

8. Coarse suspending agents generally come in particle sizes of
(please check one):

     15 to 20 millimicrons _____

     5 to 10 millimicrons _____

     $\frac{1}{2}$ to 1 millimicron _____

     15 to 20 microns _____

     5 to 10 microns _____

     $\frac{1}{2}$ to 1 micron _____

9. The slightly higher power costs associated with using Silcaspense
are offset by the fact that Silcaspense eliminates the need for
a separate production step.

     True _____

     False _____

Thank you for your help. Please fold and insert this questionnaire into your envelope. You may now leave the room. Hand the
envelope to the man at the exit door.

Follow-up Questionnaire:
With "Assumptions" to Chemists

You will recall your seeing a movie of a presentation for a new material a few weeks ago. The assumptions you were asked to make were as follows:

1. Assume you are one of a half-dozen chemists in a company manufacturing paint sold to industrial firms and to retail hardware and paint stores.
2. The product—Silcaspense, an antisettling agent—which the sales engineer in the movie offered to you is a relatively new product which is actually on the market.
3. Assume that the presentation made to you in the movie is the first time that Silcaspense was offered to your company, and that you had never before met this sales engineer.
4. Assume that your company has a group of chemists who evaluate new ingredients for your company's paints. They make the final decisions as to whether these ingredients are to replace presently used ingredients. These chemists meet as a group to make these final decisions. In short, they are group decisions. Now, assume you are a member of that group and the presentation shown in the film was made to you and *only* you in that group.

Please answer the following questions and return the questionnaire immediately in the attached self-addressed envelope.

1. Regardless of your answers on the previous questionnaire, in a meeting with your chemist colleagues with whom you jointly decide on materials changes, would you now recommend that

ABSTRACT

Industrial Purchasing Behavior
A Study of Communications Effects

This research study involved an experiment which attempted to simulate in as natural a fashion as possible some of the basic factors involved in a sales presentation of an industrial materials salesman to prospective purchasers. The experiment was carefully designed to test the applicability to purchasing decisions of concepts taken from communication theory and to distinguish among the effects on various purchasing groups of the many aspects of the selling communication.

The differential effects revealed by the experiment show the relevance to marketing managers of the varied elements of selling efforts and how they need to be considered in the formulation of marketing strategy. The study will also suggest strongly to other researchers significant new avenues for further inquiry.

The author, Theodore Levitt, is Professor of Business Administration at the Graduate School of Business Administration, Harvard University.

One of the venerable questions in marketing, and particularly the marketing of industrial products, is whether a company's generalized reputation affects its ability to sell its products. With the great flood of new products in recent years, the question has been focused more sharply around the extent to which a company's generalized reputation affects its ability to launch new products. While nobody claims that a good reputation is an adequate substitute for a good product supported by a good sales effort, the question remains as to what contribution a good reputation can make to a successful selling effort. Thus, all things being equal, does a relatively well-known company have a real edge over a relatively obscure company? Would it pay for a relatively obscure company to spend more money to advertise and promote its name and general competence or to spend more on training its salesmen?

These are some of the questions to which this monograph is addressed. The method used in the research is an outgrowth and elaboration of methods developed by behavioral scientists studying the psychology of propaganda and communication. Specifically, the objectives of the research were:

1. To determine how and to what extent source effect and sleeper effect, as conventionally defined, operate in communications between sellers and buyers of industrial products.
2. To determine whether and to what extent there is in such communications transactions a "message effect"—specifically, how the character and quality of the message impinge on source and sleeper effect.
3. To determine whether and to what extent there is in such communications transactions a "communicator effect"—specifically, whether and to what extent there is a difference between the effect of the source and the effect of the message transmitter.
4. To determine whether and to what extent there is in such communications transactions an "audience effect"—specifically, how the competence and the task of the audience impinge on communications effectiveness and how they impinge on source and sleeper effect.
5. To determine whether and to what extent in such communications transactions audience persuasibility is related (a) to how well the audience learns and retains factual information contained in the message, and (b) to how self-confident the audience is in its own reactions to the message.

The findings reported are based on a research device which attempted to simulate some of the basic factors involved in the confrontation of an industrial materials salesman and his prospects. Basically, the research involved dividing three distinctly different audiences—currently employed industrial purchasing agents, currently employed technical personnel, and full-time graduate students of business administration—into two groups each. Each of these audience groups was separately exposed to a filmed salesman's presentation for a new, technically complex ingredient used in the manufacturing of paint. There were two different versions of the filmed sales presentation, a "good" presentation and a "poor" presentation. Furthermore, both versions were varied by identifying the salesman's company as being either a "high-credibility source" (i.e., a favorably well-known firm), a "medium-credibility source," or a "low-credibility source."

Immediately following the showing of the films to the different audiences, questionnaires were filled out by the participants in the research, with a follow-up questionnaire asking for reactions five weeks later. The results were analyzed for source, presentation, audience, and sleeper effects, with special emphasis on the relation of these findings to the published findings of other communications research. The role of four variables in the respondent decision-making process were examined: respondent self-confidence, respondent trust in the message source and in the message communicator, the riskiness of the decision the respondent was asked to make, and the amount of information retained by the respondent.

The findings may be briefly summarized as follows. It seems clear that company reputation is a powerful factor in the industrial purchasing process, but that its importance varies with the technical competence and sophistication of the customer and with the personal riskiness of the decision he is expected to make. The quality of a sales message and the way it is presented are capable of moderating the influence of this "source effect," but again it varies by audience and the riskiness of the decision. Generally speaking, it pays for a company to be favorably well known, and perhaps especially among customers having some degree of technical sophistication, such as engineers and scientists. But superior sales messages and well-trained salesmen can very substantially help less well-known companies to overcome some of the disadvantages of their relative anonymity. A well-planned and well-executed direct sales presentation is a necessity for the well-known company if it is fully to *capitalize* on its reputation, but for the less well-known company it is an instrument for helping to *overcome* the disadvantage of its relative anonymity. Moreover, the greater the riskiness of the purchasing decision the customer is asked to make, the more likely is a good sales presentation to produce a customer decision in favor of the direction advocated by the source.

(Published by Division of Research, Harvard Business School, Soldiers Field, Boston, Massachusetts 02163. xv + 184 pp. $4.00. 1965) serious consideration be given to adopting the proposed material for your product? (Please check one.)

    a. Yes _____

    b. No _____

2. How confident are you of the decision you made today in answer to the above question? (Do *not* change the above answer.) Check the block on the scale below which expresses your degree of confidence to your answer to Question No. 1.

Very unconfident   Very confident

Thank you. Please return this questionnaire in the attached envelope immediately.

CHAPTER 4

Customer Decision Making:
The Presence of Source, Presentation,
Audience, and Sleeper Effects

THE OBJECTIVE of all communication is to affect its audience in some way favorable to the communicator's objective. In commercial communications, such as advertising, direct mail solicitation, and personal selling, the audience is generally a prospective customer, and it is called just that. In an important sense every statement, regardless of who makes it, addresses itself to a customer—to someone whose behavior it seeks to influence. This is true whether the communicator is a professor, a preacher, a panhandler, or a pitchman.

In commercial communications this fact is probably most clearly recognized and most widely accepted as legitimate. Everybody knows and accepts without making normative judgments that the ad man and the salesman are trying to sell something. Hence, people recognize that when the salesman finishes talking to them they must make a decision—either to reject his pleadings, to accept them, or to postpone making one of these decisions by discussing the matter further.

SOURCE AND PRESENTATION EFFECT: INITIAL AUDIENCE REACTIONS

In the present research, this fact was built into the research mechanism by giving the respondents a questionnaire immediately after the sales-presentation movie was completed and having the very first question in that questionnaire ask:

Of the chemists:	"In a meeting with your chemist colleagues with whom you jointly decide on ingredients changes, would you recommend that serious consideration be given to adopting the product presented in the movie?" (Please check one.) Yes _____ No _____
Of the purchasing agents & students:	"You must now make a choice as to whether to send the sales engineer you heard today to see one of your company's chemists. Would you send him?" (Please check one.) Yes _____ No _____

Thus, the very first question asks the respondent to make an action decision based on the movie's sales presentation. The decision to be made, however, was not the hard and difficult one of asking the respondent to purchase or even to recommend purchasing the product. It was the relatively easier one of, in effect, recommending that the product get further consideration by the company which employs him.

It will be recalled from the previous chapter that this first question was preceded by a printed repetition of the assumptions the movie asked the respondent to make regarding his job in the hypothetical company that employed him and regarding the group process by which final new-product decisions were made in the company.

Hence, the answer to the above questions imposed a minimum of risk on the respondent. He was asked, in effect, only if he thought it useful to expose others in his company to the product that was presented to him. Not surprisingly, therefore, 85.4% of all respondents answered affirmatively.

However, when this outcome is broken down by the source of the sales presentation the respondent saw, there is some modest indication of a source effect, as shown in Exhibit 4-1. Monsanto is a high-credibility source; Denver Chemical Company, a fictitious but plausible-sounding name, is a lower-credibility source; and the company whose name was not

EXHIBIT 4-1

SOURCE EFFECT: Percentage of Respondents Agreeing
to Give Product a Further Hearing, by Source
of Sales Message

Source	Favorable Responses
Monsanto	90
Denver	88
Anonymous	78
Total	85

identified (the anonymous company) presumably is the low-est credibility source. The respective proportions of affirmative answers suggest that source credibility did indeed influence the results, but only directionally. There is no significant difference between a 90% and an 88% affirmative response.

Statistically, the meaningfulness of the result becomes greater when response comparisons are made, not only in terms of the source, but also in terms of the quality of the sales presentation; that is, as between respondents who saw the "good" presentation and those who saw the "poor" presentation. This is shown in Exhibit 4-2.

EXHIBIT 4-2

SOURCE AND PRESENTATION EFFECTS: Percentage of Respondents
Agreeing to Give Product a Further Hearing, by Source
and Quality of Sales Presentation

	Presentation Quality	
Source	Good	Poor
Monsanto	96	83
Denver	94	82
Anonymous	81	74

For both the good and poor presentations, the differences between the Monsanto and the Denver results are too small to satisfy the usual tests of statistical significance, but directionally there is again the clear pattern of a declining ratio of affirmative answers as between respondent exposure to high, medium, or low-credibility sources. The binomial test, it will be recalled, is specifically useful in testing the statistical significance of results of this kind. Thus, in Exhibit 4-2 there are, for example, four ways in which the Monsanto results can be compared with the Denver and Anonymous results: (1) Monsanto-Good vs. Denver-Good; (2) Monsanto-Good vs. Anonymous-Good; (3) Monsanto-Poor vs. Denver-Poor; (4) Monsanto-Poor vs. Anonymous-Poor. In each of the four comparisons (that is, four out of four), Monsanto receives the highest percentage of affirmative answers. According to the binomial test, the probability of getting these results under an over-all probability of 0.5 is 0.0625. In other words, the observed results are not due to chance, and the probability of getting these results is not 0.5. The source effect favoring Monsanto is present at the 6.25% level of statistical significance.

Thus, whether comparing over-all results, the results only of good presentations, or only of poor presentations, source effect is clearly visible. What is even more visible from this exhibit is the fact that the affirmative response ratio of the poor presentations is consistently below that of the good presentations. In short, there is clearly a "presentation effect"; a poor presentation of the same material as that transmitted in a good presentation is less influential than a good presentation. This is hardly unexpected. Neither is it a particularly useful statement for most organizations which have an obvious practical interest in the results of source effect studies.

Source effect studies in the past have measured the effect of source credibility by holding not only the message constant but also the quality and character of its presentation. This has permitted most researchers to make relatively "clean" statements about the only factor that remained variable (the source), although Rarick [1] for the first time in 1963 seriously

---

[1] Galen R. Rarick, "Effects of Two Components of Communicator Prestige."

introduced the contaminating notion that even where the message is held constant there may be differences in audience response due to differences in the novelty or general interest evoked by the content of the message. In short, he suggested for the first time that there might be an unintentional "message effect" in the experimental design of communications research that reflects back on the credibility of the source. While communications researchers had not prior to this been oblivious to this possibility, Rarick's findings were not in the mainstream of the communications literature. Prior to Rarick's thesis, the "clean" statements by researchers have tended to produce generalizations whose practical value to the business community have been severely limited in a variety of ways. The researchers might say, for example, that a high-credibility source is more effective in producing opinion (and therefore perhaps action) change than a low-credibility source. Hence it would pay a company to cultivate a higher-credibility reputation.

But such a statement is obviously an incomplete guide to action—regardless of whether one is advising a business firm, a politician, a state propaganda agency, a charitable organization, or any other person or institution. There are a great variety of very obvious reasons for this incompleteness. One of the most important is the inescapable fact that no two communicators of the same species (two business firms, two politicians, two state propaganda agencies, etc.) will ever transmit an identical message in their attempts to influence their audiences. Two different chemical companies selling identical acrylic fibers to identical textile mills will use different words, layouts, and colors in their advertisements. Similarly, two different politicians speaking to the identical audience and holding identical views on a given issue will express their views with different arrangement of words, different speaking paces, different color and timber in their voices, different gestures, and so forth.

Hence the business firm and the propaganda agency will

want to know something more than simply that "it pays to build a high-credibility reputation." It is reasonable to assume that there are many ways in which a business firm can approach the task of influencing its prospects. Building a higher-credibility reputation through more advertising may be one way. Improving the quality and presentation of these advertisements may be another. Sending more salesmen out to call on prospects may be a third alternative. Improving the selling techniques of its salesmen may be a fourth. What all these and other possible alternatives boil down to is the question of the relationship between the power of the source effect on the one hand and available alternatives on the other.

In the case of the manufacturer of complex new products for industrial users, he knows that a personal, face-to-face sales call is a virtual necessity for getting his product adopted. One question he therefore faces ultimately comes to this: Is a good sales presentation by a salesman from a less well-known or unknown (low-credibility) firm more or less effective than a poor presentation by a well-known (high-credibility) firm? That is, all other things being equal, to what extent is it better to spend money on advertising and public relations (getting the company known favorably) rather than to spend that money on training salesmen and perfecting their sales presentations?

Exhibits 4-1 and 4-2 show the expected result that it is always better to be well-known than not well-known, and Exhibit 4-2 specifically suggests the expected result that a good sales presentation is generally better than a poor one, regardless of company reputation. A company of relatively low-credibility but making a good direct sales presentation (Anonymous = 81%) is about as effective in this instance as a high-credibility company with a poor presentation (Monsanto = 83%). A company of less than highest but more than lowest credibility (i.e., "medium" credibility, such as Denver = 94%) is decidedly more effective with a good presentation than a high-credibility company making a poor presentation (Monsanto = 83%). On the basis of these data, therefore, another way of saying the same thing is that a well-known company may not need to be as concerned with and careful about training and supervising its salesmen as a less well-known company because the former's reputation goes a long way toward preselling the salesman's product even before he reveals what it is.[2]

This generalization assumes, however, that a company's favorable well-knownness (or "high-credibility" reputation) owes nothing to the cumulative effect of past direct sales presentations—that it is entirely the result of advertising, public relations, or its generalized visibility to which the news media have in some way contributed. In the case of the present study such an assumption is at least partially warranted. The vast majority of respondents in each responding category (purchasing agents, chemists, and students) never had any direct business dealings with Monsanto, and none, of course, had any with the other two companies. Thus Monsanto's generalized reputation must be assumed to have been established not via direct experiences with Monsanto, its products, or its representatives, but via mass media and trade convention exposure by the respondents to its claims and activities.

On the basis of the above findings about the power of source effect and presentation effect, the following generalizations seem tentatively warranted:

1. It is always better to be better known than to be less well-known.

2. However, in direct industrial selling, at least in the short run, it is probably better for a new or little-known com-

---

[2] The magnitude of the favorable responses in Exhibits 4-1 and 4-2 suggest furthermore that the primary requisite for such responses by the customer is a good product—an inherently believable message. But in reality even more is involved. The role of the salesman is actually more complex, and this is examined in more detail in later sections of this chapter.

pany to spend its money on effective salesman selection and sales training than on mass media efforts to build a reputation. This conclusion is based on the high costs of advertising and especially advertising costs per relevant prospect reached relative to the incremental cost of better selection and training of salesmen.

While these generalizations have a certain general merit, the facts of industrial product selling, and particularly of new industrial product selling, require a more microscopic look at the customer decision-making unit.

SOURCE, PRESENTATION, AND AUDIENCE EFFECT: INITIAL AUDIENCE REACTIONS

The introduction of complex new products to potential industrial customers generally requires that a salesman make personal calls on the customer. But he cannot generally call directly on the person or persons who make the final purchasing decision. He is obliged first to call on a purchasing agent, who acts as a first-evaluator and screener of the product and salesman. The purchasing agent then decides whether the salesman and/or his product are to be exposed to those persons in the company who are technically more knowledgeable than the purchasing agent himself. The technical person, however, seldom makes a purchasing decision alone. He consults other technical and management personnel.

Hence it is not enough to talk about "the audience" for a sales message and the source and presentation effects of that message. It is necessary to look at audience characteristics. Exhibit 4-3 does just that.

Perhaps the most revealing fact in this exhibit is that chemists, who are technically much more knowledgeable than purchasing agents, are quite as much subject to source and to presentation effect as purchasing agents. Thus in four out of four comparisons chemists favor Monsanto over Denver and

Anonymous, indicating a Monsanto source effect at the 6.25% level of signficance via the binomial test. That is, there is only a 6.25% chance that the chemists' higher Monsanto scores are actually equal to their Denver and Anonymous scores. And, significantly, chemists are also subject to a strong presentation effect, with their percentage of affirmative responses being lower for the poor than the good presentation for each source message. One might have expected quite different responses. Since chemists are better educated technically, one might have expected that:

1. They would be less influenced by the message source—the reputation of the company which the salesman represented—and

2. They would have been less influenced by the quality of the salesman's presentation.

The somewhat unexpected results shown in Exhibit 4-3 suggest that it is just as important for the selling organization

EXHIBIT 4-3

SOURCE, PRESENTATION, AND AUDIENCE EFFECTS: Percentage of Respondents Agreeing to Give Product a Further Hearing, by Source, Quality of Sales Presentation, and Audience

	Good Presentation			Poor Presentation		
Source	Pur-chasing Agents	Chem-ists	Stu-dents	Pur-chasing Agents	Chem-ists	Stu-dents
Monsanto	96 *	96	96	76	86	85
Denver	95 *	85	100	84	60	100
Anonymous	69	86	86	59	68	91

* Note that the difference between 96% and 95% is very small, and that the base numbers on which any of the percentages in this exhibit are based were generally different from one another, though close. Hence the question arises as to how seriously one is prepared to cling to conclusions based on such a small difference and on the fact that the cells represent different numbers of respondents and different types of respondents. These issues were dealt with in the concluding four paragraphs of Chapter 3.

to build a reputation for product quality and reliability with the technically sophisticated prospects with which it hopes to deal as with the substantially less sophisticated purchasing agents who do the initial product and salesman screening. While it might *prima facie* be argued that a less sophisticated prospect can more easily be influenced by a company's reputation than a more sophisticated prospect, the fact seems to be that the sophisticated prospect can be just as vulnerable. Thus, Exhibit 4-3 shows that the Monsanto source effect is confirmed in four out of four comparisons for the technically more sophisticated chemists (in the case of the "good" presentation, 96% vs. 85% and 86%, and in the "poor" presentation 86% vs. 60% and 68%). But this source effect shows up in only three out of four comparisons for purchasing agents, yielding for the latter a 31.2% statistical significance under the binomial test. Without at this time trying to attribute too much to these differences between the results of these two "audiences," they do tend to imply that purchasing agents are actually somewhat less subject to source effect than the technically more sophisticated chemists.

Prior to the execution of this research, discussions with sales managers, advertising agency personnel, and university marketing professors yielded unqualified assertions that owing to the purchasing agents' lesser technical sophistication they would demonstrate a greater source effect—that they would rely more on company reputation than the chemists. Discussions with purchasing agents and a professor of procurement yielded assertions that purchasing agents would show less source effect. The latter seems to have been right and the former wrong. The explanation suggested by those that were right is that the sophistication that is relevant is not product or chemical sophistication but purchasing sophistication. Purchasing agents are purchasing professionals. They hear sales presentations day in and day out. They screen and buy many products. In the process they learn two important things:

1. That it is possible, in the words of one of them, "to get badly burned" by depending too much on a company's general reputation.

2. That to reduce the risk of making poor decisions they must quickly arm themselves against any gaps in their technical product sophistication by developing offsetting purchasing sophistication. The latter presumably is easier for them to develop because it is one skill whereas product sophistication requires developing skills in numerous product categories.

It is interesting to speculate why there appears to be such a widespread misconception about the relative strengths and source-effect susceptibilities of purchasing agents and technical personnel. One reason may be the general respect for and cultural bias in favor of highly educated persons, and particularly persons with technical or scientific training. All other persons in comparisons are automatically downgraded in terms of their analytical powers and capacity for objectivity. A second reason may be that the role of purchasing agents in business affairs has been widely ignored or at least assumed to be relatively minor by both business practitioners and students of business. Hence no real effort has been made to understand how they operate or how well they do their jobs. Finally, it may be that the purchasing agent, being professionally an audience for sales messages, is, as all audiences generally, viewed as a passive agent in the communications process and therefore not thought of as having a very strong will of his own. Hence he, uniquely, would be expected to be susceptible to the blandishments of a powerful communicator. Thus Bauer has pointed out that historically students of the communications process have treated the audience as a passive agent in the communications transaction, sitting fully exposed and without defenses against the communicator's intentions. Bauer has persuasively offered the counter suggestion of "The Obstinate Audience"—the audience with its own will and power of resistance.[3]

---

[3] Raymond A. Bauer, "The Obstinate Audience," 1964.

Since purchasing agents are, perhaps more than any other group in society, an audience—since that is their profession—the presumption would have been that they more than any other group are passive and defenseless objects of the communications forces arrayed against them. Hence they, more than any others, would be influenced by the powerful efforts of high-credibility communicators; they more than others would respond to the very companies which have made the greatest efforts to invest themselves with high-credibility credentials. The fact that the present research suggests that purchasing agents are not at all so pliably vulnerable to the source effect tends, on this score, to validate Bauer's obstinate audience thesis.

The indication that purchasing agents are less source-effected than chemists is validated in yet another way in Exhibit 4-3. For example, it is probably true that technical personnel (called "chemists" here for short) know more about technical products and probably know more about the character and work of the various chemicals producing companies than the average purchasing agent. This presumption is based on the fact that while purchasing agents receive salesmen and read literature from a wide variety of companies, chemists and other technical personnel are exposed to a much more limited range of companies—companies operating specifically in technical fields. Hence they would be expected to know, at least slightly better than purchasing agents, the identity, products, and competences of a good many companies producing technical products in their own and related fields. Purchasing agents would be expected to know of the larger, more visible chemical companies, but not of the smaller ones. Moreover, they would be expected to be aware of the fact that they do not know the existence or identity of the smaller companies. Hence the judgments they make about smaller plausible-sounding companies whose names they are not familiar with would be based, *ceteris paribus,* exclusively on what these companies say in their sales presentations. Yet Exhibit 4-3 shows that in the good presentation there was little difference in the affirmative response ratio as between the purchasing agents exposed to Monsanto (high-credibility source at 96%) and purchasing agents exposed to Denver (medium-credibility source at 95%), while the chemists exposed to Denver had an eleven percentage point lower affirmative score (85%) than the chemists exposed to Monsanto (96%). In other words, in this one comparison, chemists were more influenced by a high-credibility source than purchasing agents.

It can be argued, of course, that purchasing agents, being perhaps less knowledgeable about chemical companies, accepted the fictitious "Denver Chemical Company" as a plausible-sounding real company and therefore treated it the same as Monsanto. This possibility is partially supported by the peculiar purchasing agent response on the poor presentation in which Denver scored higher than Monsanto. In other words, if both companies are thought to have similar reputations, there is a greater likelihood of chance differences in respondent results. But it might also be argued that this simply confirms the fact that for the less sophisticated purchasing agents, source effect is less important since they treated the plausible-sounding medium-credibility company virtually the same as the real and well-known high-credibility company, while the sophisticated chemists treated the known company much more favorably than a company whose name they did not know and were not familiar with, no matter how plausible that name was.

It is interesting to note, however, that while purchasing agents greatly reduced their affirmative answers for the anonymous company in both the good and the poor presentation (to 69% and 59% respectively), the chemists' answers *rose* slightly from their Denver answers (to 86% for the good and 68% for the poor presentation). This may suggest the existence of a second dimension to the concept of source effect. When the source is clearly anonymous, the technically more sophisticated respondents may be more willing to take a chance on the company based on its presentation than the technically less sophisticated purchasing agents. Since, as has been concluded above, the chemists were more source-influence prone, the signal of anonymity may have cued them to the possibility of the anonymous company being well-known and therefore produced in many of them a strongly favorable result. The purchasing agents, on the other hand, while also source-influenced but generally being technically less sophisticated, in effect may have been reluctant to take a chance on their being able to rely so fully on their ability to judge the message by itself. Therefore they reduced their risk of error by simply rejecting the anonymous company more completely.

The results of the students' reactions are not so clear cut. In each case Denver scores better than either Monsanto or Anonymous. This may, as with purchasing agents, reflect their lesser knowledge not just about chemical companies, but about business firms in general. To them the "Denver Chemical Company" probably sounded like a much more plausibly real company than Monsanto, even though the latter was real and the former fictitious. While this interpretation of student results is purely speculative and generally lacking in a strong rationale, no other explanation seems apparent nor does the result by itself seem significant.

SOURCE AND PRESENTATION EFFECT: RESPONSIBLE AUDIENCE REACTIONS

The preceding analysis has been on questions in which respondents were asked merely whether they would recommend giving the product a further hearing in their companies; i.e., whether they would refer it to others or simply dismiss it as being of no further interest. They were not asked to assume any personal responsibility for actually adopting the product. Hence they were being asked to make relatively low-risk de-

cisions. The question therefore is: What would have been the
outcome under requirements to make substantially higher-risk
decisions—decisions in which they were required to assume
full responsibility for adopting the product?

The answer is provided by the responses to the following
questions asked later in the questionnaire:

Of the chemists: "Suppose you had full responsibility in your
                     company to make the decision as to whether
                     your company switches to the product the
                     sales engineer offered? Would you switch?"
                     Yes _____ No _____
Of the purchasing   "Suppose instead of sending the sales engi-
agents & students: neer to the chemist, you had *full* responsi-
                     bility in your company to make the decision
                     as to whether your company switches to the
                     product the sales engineer offered. Would you
                     switch?"
                     Yes _____ No _____

Exhibit 4-4 shows the consolidated percentage "yes" answers to these questions in Column 3, and compares them in
Column 2 with the "yes" answers to the earlier question in
which the respondents were asked only whether they would
give the product a further hearing in their company. Thus
Column 2 repeats the results listed in Exhibit 4-1, which are
here designated as "referral" responses, and Column 3 figures
are the "yes" answers to the above questions as a percentage
of those who said "yes" to the earlier questions whose answers
are tabulated in Column 2. (These are designated as "adoption" responses.) In short, the 40% in Column 3 is 40% of
90% in Column 2.

The affirmative adoption ratios in Column 3 again show
the existence of source effect. The Monsanto score is above
both Denver and Anonymous, although there is little difference between the scores of the latter two companies in this

EXHIBIT 4-4

SOURCE EFFECT: Percentage of Respondents Agreeing to a Further
Hearing for the Product, and Percentage Adopting the Product
with Sole Responsibility for Adoption Decision, by Source

Source	Referral *	Adoption †	Attrition in Affirmative Responses
(1)	(2)	(3)	(4) = 100% − Col. 3
Monsanto	90	40	60
Denver	88	35	65
Anonymous	78	34	66

* The column is a repetition of Exhibit 4-1. "Referral" refers to answers to the question of whether, on first being presented with the new
product, respondents would give it a further hearing in their firms by referring it to others under conditions in which the respondents assumed no
personal responsibility for making the product adoption decision.

† The column represents that proportion of respondents in Column 2
who said later in the questionnaire that, if they had sole responsibility for
deciding whether the product was to be adopted, they would adopt it.

high-risk situation in which respondents were asked to make
adoption decisions strictly on their sole initiative and without
sharing responsibility with others.

Respondents are clearly concerned with personal risk-reduction. The greater their personal risk in making a buying decision, the less likely they are to decide so quickly.[4] A comparison of Columns 2 and 3 clearly shows that when respondents
were asked to assume the greater risk of taking full responsibility for adopting the product, a great many of them refused
to do so. Of those who saw the Monsanto presentation and
who were willing to give the product a further hearing at the
outset, only 40% were willing to adopt it on their own initiative and with sole responsibility for doing so. In short, there
was a 60% attrition of favorable ("yes") responses as between the two kinds of actions they were asked to take; that
is, an additional hearing in which others were in effect ex-

[4] See Raymond A. Bauer, "Consumer Behavior as Risk-Taking," 1960.

pected to make the adoption decision versus making it themselves. Moreover, as the attrition tabulation of Column 4
shows, under high-risk conditions (adoption) there is a somewhat greater attrition of favorable responses for the low-
credibility sources than the high-credibility source (65% and
66% vs. 60%). What this means is that source effect is more
effective in the adoption situation than in the mere referral situation. When it comes to taking higher personal risks, at least
as shown in the present case, respondents tend more to depend
on the credibility of the source in making their decisions.
That is, when looking at the combined results of the three
types of audiences used in the present research, the conclusion
seems to be that it is somewhat more useful to have a good
company reputation in order to get product adoption than
merely to get a favorable first hearing. While this tends to conflict with the views of Bauer,[5] it will be seen later that differences in the reactions of different audiences may in important
cases sustain Bauer's position.

Exhibit 4-5 divides the result of Exhibit 4-4 by the quality
of the sales presentation. The same general pattern exists in

EXHIBIT 4-5

SOURCE AND PRESENTATION EFFECTS: Percentage of Affirmative
Referral and Adoption Respondents, by Source and Quality of
Sales Presentation

	Good Presentation			Poor Presentation		
Source	Refer-ral	Adop-tion	Attri-tion *	Refer-ral	Adop-tion	Attri-tion *
Monsanto	96	49	51	83	27	73
Denver	94	48	52	82	18	82
Anonymous	81	45	55	74	22	78

* See Exhibit 4-4.

[5] Raymond A. Bauer, "Risk Handling in Drug Adoption: The Role of
Company Preference," 1961. Bauer concludes that source effect is more important in low-risk situations.

the "adoption" results as was noted earlier (Exhibit 4-2) in connection with "referral" results. Source effect in favor of Monsanto is present in four out of four comparisons, for a 6.25% level of statistical significance. But there is one very notable difference between this exhibit and Exhibit 4-2; namely, that the previously noted depressing power of a poor presentation is substantially stronger in adoption than in referral decisions. Thus, in the case of Monsanto, the poor presentation in the referral test produces a fading of affirmative responses from 96% to 83%, but in the adoption test affirmative responses collapse from 49% to 27%. The average attrition ratio between referral and adoption responses rose from 53% for all the good presentations to 74% for all the poor presentations. In other words, as might be expected, a poor presentation hurts the seller more when he is addressing the ultimate sole decision maker than when he is addressing the same individual who is acting as an intermediary. It is probably also safe to generalize this statement to say that when addressing the ultimate sole decision maker it is substantially more important to make a good presentation than when addressing an intermediary. In order to get a first hearing for a new product, it seems less important to have a good presentation than when attempting to get an adoption.

Summarizing Exhibit 4-5, the following conclusions seem warranted:

1. In order to get a favorable audience response it is better for a company to be better known than to be less well-known or anonymous.

2. In general this may be slightly more true to get a direct product adoption than merely to get a favorable first hearing and referral.

3. A good presentation produces a much greater favorable response than a poor one and it has its greatest positive impact when people are asked to act with full responsibility on them personally—when their risk is higher. A good presentation

always helps, but it helps much more to get product adoption than to get a favorable first hearing. Thus it clearly pays to get the best "presenters" to those meetings or sales situations at which decision makers are present—to marshal the best men for the crucial situations.

4. In first-hearing situations (referral), a poor presentation by a well-known company may be less effective than a good presentation by a less well-known company (83% vs. 94%), but it may be as good as a good presentation by an anonymous one (83% vs. 81%). However, to get favorable action in final decision-making situations (adoption), a good presentation by an anonymous company is much better than a poor one by a well-known company (45% of 81% = 36% vs. 27% of 83% = 22%). Hence, face-to-face presentation is more important in the final analysis than advertising or public relations.

5. Regardless of whether a presentation is for an initial hearing or to get final product adoption, a poor presentation results in substantial loss of sales effectiveness.

6. To get an initially favorable hearing (referral), better sales training (as a means of getting a better presentation) by a medium- or low-reputation (low-credibility) company may be somewhat better than less well-trained salesmen representing a known company, but this is not clearly validated (94% vs. 83%). However, to get product adoption, good training by a low-reputation company is strongly superior to inadequate training by a high-reputation company (48% and 45% vs. 27%). In any case, reputation helps greatly.

SOURCE, PRESENTATION, AND AUDIENCE EFFECT: RESPONSIBLE
AUDIENCE REACTIONS

Exhibits 4-4 and 4-5 showed clearly that when faced with the greater risk of assuming full personal responsibility for adopting a new product, the purchaser (audience) greatly reduces his willingness to support that product. Moreover, when he does support the product, he relies more heavily on the quality of the sales presentation than on the vendor's reputation. The question now remains how this behavior varies as between buyers with more or less product sophistication. The answer lies in an examination of Exhibit 4-6. (The upper panel of this exhibit—"referral"—is a repetition of Exhibit 4-3.)

EXHIBIT 4-6

SOURCE, PRESENTATION, AND AUDIENCE EFFECTS: Percentage of Affirmative Referral and Adoption Respondents, by Quality of Sales Presentation and by Audience

	Good Presentation			Poor Presentation		
Audience	Purchasing Agents	Chemists	Students	Purchasing Agents	Chemists	Students
	(1)	(2)	(3)	(4)	(5)	(6)
			Referral			
Monsanto	96	96	96	76	86	85
Denver	95	89	100	84	60	100
Anonymous	69	86	86	59	68	91
			Adoption			
Monsanto	36	42	70	15	33	29
Denver	50	41	50	19	25	14
Anonymous	36	37	58	20	14	28

The expected fact that emerges from Exhibit 4-6 is that all three audiences greatly reduced their affirmative responses when asked to act with solid personal responsibility for adopting the product. Indeed, while a majority of each of the 18 referral audiences said "yes," they would give a product a further hearing, in only 2 of these 18 audiences did a majority say "yes," they would personally adopt the product (70% and 58%). That is, in 16 of the 18 adoption audiences, half or more respondents said "no," they would not adopt, even though all of these had said "yes," they would give it a further hearing and refer it onward. Responsibility produces extreme caution.

But the extent to which this risk-reducing behavior exists varies by the message source (vendor) and the audience. Thus there is a Monsanto-favoring (high-credibility) source effect, but it is confined largely to chemists and students, neither of which are professional purchasers. Combining the good and poor adoption presentations, chemists and students gave Monsanto a higher percentage of affirmative responses in eight out of eight cases, supporting the existence of a Monsanto source effect at the 0.4% level of significance. There is only a 0.4% probability that the higher chemist and student responses for Monsanto are actually equal to their Denver and Anonymous responses.

By contrast, purchasing agents displayed no Monsanto-favoring source effect in the adoption situations, while showing a clear (though less than the chemists) source effect in the less risky referral cases.[6] As noted before, when it comes to making a high-risk decision, purchasing agents discount the reputation of the seller much more than less sophisticated purchasers (chemists and students), even though they themselves may have less product sophistication. In spite of their higher product sophistication, chemists are more influenced by the seller's reputation.

The extent to which this is true in adoption decisions is quite remarkable. Thus in the lower panel of Exhibit 4-6 it will be seen that while purchasing agents *never* reduce their willingness to buy as between Monsanto on the one hand and Denver and Anonymous on the other, for either the good or the poor presentation (Col. 1, 36% vs. 50% and 36%, and Col. 4, 15% vs. 19% and 20%), chemists *always* reduce their willingness to buy (Cols. 2 and 5). Exactly what caused these differences is not clear. One possibility is that with chemists

---

[6] Indeed, there seems to be a slight tendency for purchasing agents to disfavor Monsanto relative to Denver and Anonymous (50% and 36% vs. 36% in good presentations and 19% and 20% vs. 15% in poor presentations). This phenomenon is discussed below.

(that is, the technically sophisticated audience) there is a double source effect—one in referral decisions and then a second additive one in adoption decisions. But with purchasing agents there is source effect in referral decisions and not additionally in adoption decisions. The reason purchasing agents experience no additional source effect in adoption decisions is perhaps because such decisions are not part of their ordinary function. But for respondents who ordinarily have adoption-decision responsibilities, the additional influence of source credibility merely reflects how their role influences their perception and their behavior.

Exhibit 4-6 also suggests that the powerful influence of the previously mentioned purchasing (audience) professionalism on the behavior of purchasing agents (as opposed to the influence of product professionalism) may actually produce a reverse source effect. Thus the lower panel of Columns 1 and 4 shows that of those respondents who would refer the salesman onward to begin with, there was actually a tendency of purchasing agents to *favor* the less well-known companies when asked to assume full adoption responsibility, and particularly in the case of poor presentations (Col. 4). Although this result is contrary to the expectations of the advertising experts, sales managers, and marketing professors that were interviewed as part of the present research, it is consistent with the expectations of many purchasing executives and of at least one well-known procurement professor. The latter contended that purchasing agents, being professional buyers who are exposed to numerous salesmen each week, learn to discount the effects of source, and do so increasingly as the risk of the decision gets higher. But beyond that, it was asserted that they learn to discount the flaws and flattery in a salesman's presentation technique and actually tend unconsciously to "help" or "favor" a salesman from a less well-known company who makes a poor presentation. It was argued that they may think of him as being at a disadvantage and of being in trouble and therefore they might unconsciously help him out. Since the purchasing agents are professionals, they see his flaws and understand his problems and therefore automatically try to see how his effectiveness could be improved. In the process they in effect "improve" it themselves by "giving him a break" in their behavior toward him.

Whether this argument about the effect of purchasing professionalism is entirely acceptable may be questionable. For one thing, the results might be a matter of status or role empathy. In many firms, although increasingly in fewer in recent years, purchasing agents occupy a relatively low place in the corporate status hierarchy. It might therefore be argued that it generally would be natural for them to tend to sympathize with representatives from lower status (less well-known) companies. But this is a highly speculative proposition.

A much more plausible and less involved explanation for purchasing agents appearing to favor the less well-known companies is that they simply see these companies as potential competitors of the known companies. Encouraging such companies encourages competition among suppliers, thus ultimately helping the purchaser.

But none of this alters the continuing strong evidence of a powerful presentation effect and its varying impact as between audiences. Exhibit 4-6 shows that contrary to the referral results, in adoption situations any good presentation by any less well-known company always outperformed all poor presentations of any well-known company. No good-presentation affirmative ratio was lower than any poor-presentation affirmative ratio. Given the present experiment's range of differences between the "good" and "poor" presentations, and between "high" and "low" credibility sources, it can be said that when it comes to making an actual sale (or achieving the final decisive influence that produces concrete action), there is no substitute for a good presentation, regardless of the source's reputation (credibility).

SLEEPER EFFECT: INITIAL AND RESPONSIBLE AUDIENCE REACTIONS

Rarely does a prospect place an order for a new technical product the first time a salesman calls on him. He neither does this nor is expected to do it. Whether he does indeed place an order later is very much related to the extent to which his original favorable reaction endured or the extent to which his unfavorable reaction changed—that is, to the extent that there is a positive or a negative sleeper effect. Exhibit 4-7 shows the results to the following "referral" question that was asked of all respondents five weeks after they answered the original questionnaire:

Of the chemists:	"Regardless of your answers on the previous questionnaire, in a meeting with your chemist colleagues with whom you jointly decide on materials changes, would you now recommend that serious consideration be given to adopting the proposed material for your product?" Yes _____ No _____
Of the purchasing agents & students:	"Regardless of your answers on the previous questionnaire, would you now send the sales engineer to see one of your company's chemists?" Yes _____ No _____

Exhibit 4-7 shows that of the respondents who on the original questionnaire answered "yes" to both the referral and the adoption questions, 96% answered "yes" on the five-week follow-up referral question and 4% completely changed their minds and answered "no." While ordinarily it might be argued that 96% is an extremely strong indication of response stability, it is important to recognize exactly what the residual 4% represents. It represents respondents who five weeks earlier had answered "yes" to the high-risk, adoption question, but now refused to answer "yes" when asked merely whether they would *refer* it on to others. It is possible to argue that this 4% is an unexpectedly high figure given the differences in as-

EXHIBIT 4-7

SLEEPER EFFECT: Follow-up Response Percentages,
by Adoption and Referral Responses

	Adoption/Referral Response Categories *		
Follow-up *Response*	*Referral–Yes* *Adoption–Yes*	*Referral–Yes* *Adoption–No*	*Referral–No* *Adoption–No*
(1)	(2)	(3)	(4)
Yes	96	85	28
No	4	15	72

* The 96 in Column 2 means that of the respondents who answered
"yes" to both the referral and adoption questions, 96% said "yes" in the
referral follow-up questionnaire they answered five weeks later. The number of respondents involved were: Col. 2, 112; Col. 3, 186; Col. 4, 47.

sumptions. Since it probably took a great deal of courage to
respond affirmatively on the original adoption decision, to
then refuse even to simply refer it to others later implies a
more than 180° shift in subsequent opinion and self-confidence. To this extent, the shift is not merely evidence of sleeper
effect, but of *negative* sleeper effect. Previous research in this
area of communications would have predicted a change in actions but probably not from a "yes" in a high-risk situation to
a "no" in a low-risk situation. It is of course possible to attribute the 4% switch to attenuation of interest, especially in view
of the elapsed time, with a resulting regression effect or an increase in random behavior on the part of the subjects. This is
entirely possible, though it does not clearly show up in the self-
confidence that respondents had in these responses. (See Chapter 5.)

In view of the 4% figure, regardless of its actual significance, it is not surprising to find that the proportion of those
who changed their minds increased even more (to 15%, Col.
3) among those who originally said "yes," they would refer it
onward, but "no," they would not adopt it under conditions of
having to take sole responsibility for such a decision. But

there is one more surprise in the results. Column 4 shows that of those who rejected the product originally in *both* the referral and the adoption situations, 28% later accepted it under referral conditions. Such strong original feelings might have led one to expect much less subsequent opinion-action change.

Thus, among persons who make either a strong or even a partial gesture toward accepting the product originally, there is a follow-up, or sleeper, attrition in inverse proportion to the extent of their original support of the product. The greater the original commitment to the product, the less the subsequent attrition. However, among those completely rejecting the original sales approach, there is a strong tendency to give it a further hearing later.[7] All three categories of respondents suffer from a form of cognitive dissonance [8] which causes them somewhat to change their minds later. But the group which was most certain about fully rejecting the product at first seems to have been most bothered about its original decision and most likely to reverse itself. Moreover, the combination of its two original negative decisions was so strong that the opportunity for regress was great.

It would seem therefore that a consistent "no" response to the inaugural sales presentation created more of an opportunity for later persuading the respondent to reconsider his decision than a vacillating response in the inaugural presentation. But in all cases there is a tendency to change responses with the passage of time.

The research also sought to determine the extent to which these sleeper-effect shifts were related to source and presentation influences. Indications in Exhibit 4-8 are that these influences were too slight to warrant discussions. However, the ex-

---

[7] This finding is quite unexpected and potentially very significant for selling strategy. Further research should be directed toward seeing if these results are repeated.

[8] Leon Festinger, *A Theory of Cognitive Dissonance,* 1957.

EXHIBIT 4-8

SLEEPER, SOURCE, AND PRESENTATION EFFECTS: Original
and Follow-up Referral Response Percentages, by Source
and Quality of Sales Presentation

	Original–Yes Follow-up–Yes		*Original–Yes Follow-up–No*	
Source	*Good Presentation*	*Poor Presentation*	*Good Presentation*	*Poor Presentation*
Monsanto	88	71	7	12
Denver	90	67	6	14
Anonymous	73	70	9	5

hibit also shows that people who saw the good Denver and
good Anonymous presentations registered a higher percentage of "yes" answers on the follow-up, and a lower percentage
of shifts to "no" answers than did the viewers of the poor Monsanto presentations. By the binomial test, a higher performance is indicated by the good presentations of Denver and
Anonymous over the poor presentation of Monsanto in four
out of four cases. This indicates, at the 6.25% significance
level, that a good presentation by a less well-known company may be more durable and more effective with the passage of time than a poor presentation by a well-known company.

These shifts in responses again validate Rarick's contention
about the multidimensional character of what Hovland, Weiss,
and Kelman called source effect. Source is not a "clean" and
unidimensional influence phenomenon. Indeed, presentation is
so powerful that it is important for students of the source effect phenomenon to avoid appearing to overemphasize its importance in communications. Since in real life no two sources
ever transmit the same information in the same way, no person
would deny that presentation must have its influence. Hence it
is essential when measuring source effect always to attempt to
understand the absolute contribution of presentation effect to

a source-effect coefficient. And the same applies to sleeper effect.

Moreover, the role of the audience in source, presentation, and sleeper effect appears to be more powerful and significant than has been generally emphasized. The published Hovland, Weiss, and Kelman studies have been based on experiments with college students, generally students in psychology courses. Even though one might argue that these experiments used topics that made sense with students, one of the things which stands out clearly in the present research is how widely student responses can vary from nonstudent responses. For example, Exhibit 4-6 shows a very peculiar student response pattern compared to purchasing agents and chemists. It is interesting to speculate about comparing the kind of advice one might give to businessmen based on a study using only students versus a study using only purchasing agents or only chemists, or both purchasing agents and chemists combined into a single audience.

Even using only students can, by itself, be enormously misleading about how "students" react. For example, in Exhibit 4-6, Column 6 shows an extraordinary difference in student source effect results as between referral and adoption responses. The results are totally erratic. On the basis of this, would one conclude that there is no source effect? On the basis of the findings of this and other research the answer is "no." Then why such odd results in the present case? Perhaps it is that the experiment asked students to assume a role they did not really understand. It may also have been the composition of the student group and, indeed, the fact that the respondents were students. For example, while all the students were volunteers and graduate business school students, about 40% held undergraduate degrees in science, mathematics, or engineering, and the rest in liberal arts. Moreover, nearly half had full-time business experience and the rest had no such experience. Hence, the student audience composition may have greatly affected the research results, just as any other audience composition clearly does. Furthermore, composition is more than a matter of background. In the present research, the students were unique in that for two concentrated months prior to their being exposed to the sales presentations they had been rigorously drilled in the analysis of business problems, with particular emphasis on recognizing inconsistencies in business practices and in business people's behavior. This disciplining may very well have made this student audience quite different from other student audiences.

These findings about the peculiarities of student responses suggest that one should advise extreme caution in generalizing to the business community on the basis of communications research involving student subjects. Indeed, the pioneers in this kind of research have been extremely careful about making any kinds of generalizations. If there is any danger of over-generalization in this or other aspects of their findings, it certainly does not lie with them.

CHAPTER 5

Decision-Making Variables:
The Roles of Self-Confidence, Trust, Risk,
and Information Retention

A VARIETY of communications researches have shown that source effect is very much a matter of the perceived trustworthiness of the source. Hovland, Weiss, and Kelman are particularly associated with this finding, having shown that audience opinion change tends strongly to be in the direction of the position advocated by a high-trust source.[1] Research by Cox found that the likelihood of opinion change, and therefore the stability of the original and the subsequent opinion, is a function of the subject's confidence in the specific opinion he holds and in his generalized self-confidence in himself.[2] Janis and others also demonstrated that persons with little generalized self-confidence tended to be more persuasible than persons with more self-confidence.[3] This means that while an examina-

---

[1] Carl I. Hovland and Walter Weiss, "The Influence of Source Credibility on Communications Effectiveness," 1951; Herbert C. Kelman and Carl I. Hovland, " 'Reinstatement' of the Communicator in Delayed Measurement of Opinion Change," 1953. See also David H. Kulp, II, "Prestige as Measured by Single Experience Changes and Their Permanency," 1934, and A. O. Bowden, Floyd F. Caldwell, and Guy A. West, "A Study in Prestige," 1934.

[2] Donald R. Cox, *Information and Uncertainty: Their Effects on Consumers' Product Evaluations,* 1963.

[3] Irving L. Janis, "Personality Correlates of Susceptibility to Persuasion," 1954; Irving L. Janis and Seymour Feshback, "Personality Differences Associated with Responsiveness to Fear-Arousing Communications," 1954.

tion of people's opinion changes that are associated with messages from various sources may provide clues regarding what
actions they will take, it tells nothing about the stability of either their opinions or their subsequent actions.

In this connection, Bauer has referred to the obstinate audience [4] not only as a way of highlighting the audience's capacity for resisting sales messages, but also to dramatize its
multidimensionality. Some audience members may be more
easily persuaded than others. But perhaps even more important, and certainly more subtle, is the fact that while two persons may be influenced in the same direction and, subsequent
to a message, now hold a new view, one may hold it more
firmly than another and therefore be more readily vulnerable
either to the sleeper effect or to counterpersuasion. The power
of counterpersuasion as an important force whose influence
must be understood in any statement of source effect has been
most recently demonstrated in a study by Hilibrand,[5] who has
shown that the presumed authoritativeness of a message source
greatly influences respondents' subsequent susceptibilities to
counterpersuasion.

All this means that the study results discussed in the previous chapter must be examined in further depth. Specifically,
with what degree of self-confidence did the respondents take
the two actions they were asked to take—namely, to give the
product a further hearing by referring it onward to others, or
to adopt it directly? How did their self-confidences vary by
whether they accepted or rejected the product? How did they
vary by the source and by the quality of the sales presentation?
To what extent did a respondent's trust in the salesman condition his answers? What were the ingredients of trust? How did
all these variables affect the ultimate duration of a respondent's
original decisions—that is, how were they related to the sleeper
effect?

---

4 *Loc. cit.*

5 Murray Hilibrand, *Source Credibility and the Persuasive Process,* 1964.

SELF-CONFIDENCE AND DECISION RISKS: ORIGINAL RESPONSES

In the present research, each time respondents were required to make a choice in connection with the product presented to them in the film, they were asked to indicate the confidence they had in the decision they had just made. Thus, after being asked whether they would give the product a further hearing, they were immediately asked the following question:

> "How confident are you in the decision you made in answer to the above question? (Do *not* change the above answer.) On the following scale, place a check mark within the block which expresses the degree of confidence you have in your response to Question No. 1."

In scoring the results, a check mark was given a number from 1 to 9 corresponding to the block, reading from left to right, in the above nine-point scale. Exhibit 5-1 shows the average scores for both the referral and the adoption answers, by source and quality of the sales presentation. The higher the average score, the higher the respondents' ratings of their confidences in their answers.

Examining first only the referral results (upper panel), it is clear that the self-confidence scores do not show much of a source-effect in favor of Monsanto, the well-known company. If anything, people saying "yes," they would give the product a further hearing, indicated less confidence when exposed to the Monsanto presentations than to Denver or Anonymous. "No" answers showed no significant source effect in any direction. Since the question in connection with which respondents were required to rate their confidences in their answers imposed little personal responsibility on the respondents (they were asked whether they would suggest the product be given

EXHIBIT 5-1

RESPONDENT SELF-CONFIDENCE SCORES: Self-Confidence
of Respondents to Referral and Adoption Questions,
by Source and Quality of Sales Presentation

	Good Presentation			Poor Presentation		
Response	Mon-santo	Den-ver	Anony-mous	Mon-santo	Den-ver	Anony-mous
Referral						
"Yes," would give product further hearing	7.2	7.5	7.5	6.7	6.6	7.0
"No," would not give product further hearing	8.0	7.3	7.9	6.8	6.9	6.8
Adoption						
"Yes," would adopt the product	5.7	6.1	5.2	5.9	6.0	5.7
"No," would not adopt the product	7.1	6.7	6.6	7.1	6.7	6.9

another hearing rather than whether they would directly adopt
it), the resulting self-confidence ratings would not be expected to discriminate very much, especially as between presentation sources.

But in referral situations they did discriminate as between
presentation qualities, a result which seems reasonable. Indeed,
the quality of the presentation strongly affects the confidence
respondents have in their answers, regardless of whether they
answer "for" or "against" the product. A good presentation,
regardless of source and regardless of the respondent's answer,
generates greater self-confidence in an answer than a poor
presentation. The lowest good-presentation score (7.2) is
above the highest poor-presentation score (7.0), and in every
matched cell the good-presentation score is above its compara-
ble poor-presentation score. Moreover, little difference exists
between confidence scores on "yes" and "no" answers.

This suggests that, in referral situations, while a good presentation always yields more self-confidence in the respondent's answer, it is also a double-edged sword that strikes in both directions since the negative respondents are just as sure of themselves as the positive respondents, and vice versa.

This finding raises interesting questions about audience behavior. For example, it is understandable that the confidence scores associated with the "yes" good-presentation are higher than those of the "yes" poor-presentation. The good presentation clearly makes the affirmative respondent more sure of his answer than does the poor presentation. But if that is so, why among negative referral responses should the good presentation also outscore the poor presentation? One might argue, without regard to the proportions of respondents influenced in one or the other direction, that if the "yes" score is higher on the good presentation, then the poor presentation "no's" would score higher on the poor presentation than on the good one. This would follow because a poor presentation presumably gives less effective assurance to the respondent that he should support the product. What seems to have happened, however, is that cause-and-effect worked differently as between good vs. poor presentations on the one hand and "yes"-vs.-"no" answers to the particular presentation on the other hand. Thus it may be that while higher confidences are *produced* by better presentations, apparently higher confidences are *required* to say "no" to these presentations. A good presentation is more effective than a poor one, but in either case "no" answers within a presentation category may require more self-confidence to say "no."

This point seems to be clearly validated in the confidence scores associated with the question that required the respondents to make decisions regarding the product's actual adoption rather than simply to decide whether to refer it onward for a further hearing. In other words, when respondents were clearly required to take a higher personal risk, their "no" decisions clearly had higher self-confidence scores. This is demonstrated in the lower panel of Exhibit 5-1.

This panel shows that in high-risk situations (with responsibility) in all categories the respondents were always more confident in their "no" answers than in their "yes" answers. And Exhibit 5-2 strengthens this finding substantially by showing that this unqualified pattern also held for each audience category of each source message. By the binomial test the higher confidences of "no" answers in 18 of 18 comparisons in Exhibit 5-2 indicates a significance level of 0.001%. Without qualification this means that all groups are less certain about making a decision to buy a product than not to buy it, to hold opinions favorable to the communicator than unfavorable to him.

Thus while the confidence scores to the referral question (upper panel, Exhibit 5-1) showed an ambiguous pattern between "no"-vs.-"yes" responses, perhaps mildly but not sig-

EXHIBIT 5-2

RESPONDENT SELF-CONFIDENCE SCORES: Self-Confidence
of Respondents to Adoption Question, by Source,
Quality of Sales Presentation, and Audience *

Adoption Answer, by Audience		Good Presentation			Poor Presentation		
		Mon-santo	Den-ver	Anony-mous	Mon-santo	Den-ver	Anony-mous
Purchasing Agents	Yes	6.1	7.2	6.8	5.5	5.7	5.5
	No	7.6	7.5	8.4	7.5	7.6	7.9
Chemists	Yes	5.4	5.4	6.1	6.0	6.3	6.0
	No	7.1	7.0	6.2	7.2	6.8	6.6
Students	Yes	5.6	5.7	4.3	6.0	4.7	5.7
	No	6.4	5.8	5.1	6.8	6.1	6.3

* Includes only those respondents who said "yes" to the referral question tabulated in Exhibit 5-1.

nificantly showing higher scores for the "no" respondents, under adoption conditions (lower panel, Exhibit 5-1, and Exhibit 5-2) the pattern is unmistakable. People are more sure about their "no" than their "yes" answers. This suggests that the more the personal risk, the more persuasion it probably takes to get the customer (audience) to switch, in effect, from an existing product (opinion). Put another way, the more the personal risk the more confident the customer (audience) is that it is less risky not to change from a given product (or opinion) than to change. Hence, it would appear that once the customer (audience) has made a decision in an adoption situation, the seller (communicator) has greater difficulty both in getting the negative respondent to change his mind and in keeping the affirmative respondent from changing his mind. The affirmative respondent is less sure of himself than the negative respondent.

The important role that risk-taking plays in the respondent's behavior is further illustrated by Exhibit 5-3. This shows the confidence scores to the referral question for respondents who

EXHIBIT 5-3

RESPONDENT SELF-CONFIDENCE SCORES: Self-Confidence Scores of Referral "Yes" Respondents, by Response to Adoption Question, by Source, Quality of Sales Presentation, and Audience

Adoption Answer, by Audience		Good Presentation			Poor Presentation		
		Mon-santo	Den-ver	Anony-mous	Mon-santo	Den-ver	Anony-mous
Purchasing							
Agents	Yes	7.4	7.7	7.7	4.0	6.3	8.0
	No	8.3	7.4	8.9	8.1	7.2	7.1
Chemists	Yes	6.9	8.0	7.9	7.2	7.7	6.5
	No	7.4	7.5	6.8	5.7	5.1	6.6
Students	Yes	7.3	8.0	7.5	7.6	7.7	8.0
	No	4.7	6.7	6.7	6.3	6.5	6.7

answered this question "yes" and breaks these respondents down to whether they answered the subsequent adoption question as "yes" or "no." The exhibit shows that respondents who said "yes," they would adopt the product directly by themselves, generally had higher confidence scores on their original referral "yes" answers than those who said "no," they would not adopt it by themselves. This occurred in 12 of 18 cases, for a significance level of 11.9%. In short, persons with less confidence in their original affirmative low-risk referral decisions were, expectedly, more likely to shift to "no" responses in their subsequent high-risk adoption decisions. Both the "yes" and the "no" high-risk respondents made their decisions in directions consistent with their earlier states of confidence in less risky decisions regarding the same product. In other words, the degree of self-confidence an audience has in its affirmative decision in a low-risk situation may for some purposes be an excellent predictor of its decision in an identical high-risk situation.

Exhibit 5-3 also again validates the power of source effect. In 11 out of 12 comparisons persons who said "yes," they would adopt the product, had less confidence in their original referral "yes" answers for Monsanto than they did for Denver or Anonymous. Thus the "yes" adoption answer tended more easily to be given by persons who started out requiring less self-confidence to support Monsanto even under a low-risk situation. Monsanto did not require high self-confidence for respondents to favor it.

No significant audience effect was present in these answers, but there was a presentation effect. Comparing good-vs.-poor presentations, in 7 out of 9 cases people answering "no," they would not adopt, had more confidence in their original "yes" referral answers on good presentations than on poor presentations. This is significant at the 9.0% level and suggests that to switch to a "no" answer meant, not that it took more confidence in the respondent's original answer, but only that when

EXHIBIT 5-4

RESPONDENT SELF-CONFIDENCE SCORES: Differences in Scores
Between Referral and Adoption "Yes" Respondents, by
Source, Quality of Sales Presentation, and Audience *

| | Good Presentation | | | Poor Presentation | | |
Audience	Mon-santo	Den-ver	Anony-mous	Mon-santo	Den-ver	Anony-mous
Purchasing Agents	1.3	0.5	1.0	(1.5)	0.7	2.5
Chemists	1.5	2.6	1.7	1.2	1.3	0.5
Students	1.7	2.3	3.2	1.6	3.0	2.3

* Average confidence scores on the adoption question have been sub-
tracted from average confidence scores on the referral question. Parentheses
indicate that the adoption confidence score was higher than the referral
confidence score.

he was exposed to a good presentation it took more confidence
in that original answer in order for him to switch later. Moreover, the better information he received in the "good" presentations gave him this confidence. "Yes" answers showed no
such effect. This means, as has been shown before, that the
good presentation is more of a double-edged sword, cutting
powerfully in both directions, than the poor presentation.
From the communicator's viewpoint, though a good presentation is more effective in getting desired results than a poor
presentation, it is also less predictable in the sense that one
cannot be sure it will not also hurt. The poor presentation is
more predictable in that it generally always hurts and never
helps.

The importance of risk-taking in determining a respondent's
behavior can, finally, be shown in yet another way. Exhibit
5-4 shows the difference in confidence scores between respondents who answered "yes" to both the referral and the adoption
questions. It is the result of subtracting the adoption from the
referral scores. A positive number indicates that the average
adoption confidence score was lower than the average referral
score. A negative number indicates the opposite. Thus in 17

of 18 comparisons the adoption scores were lower than the referral scores, yielding a binomial significance of 0.001%. A
comparison of the upper and lower panels of Exhibit 5-1
shows the same pattern among the "yes" referral respondents
who said "no" to the adoption question. In short, high-risk decision situations are generally accompanied by lower self-
confidence scores in the decisions that are rendered.

While no source effect was evident in referral confidence
scores (upper panel, Exhibit 5-1), other measures reveal a
source effect in favor of Monsanto. It shows up particularly in
the "yes" adoption percentages in the lower panel of Exhibit
5-1 (6 out of 8 comparisons favor Monsanto), and in Exhibit
4-4 (Chapter 4), but only slightly in the Exhibit 5-4 comparison of referral and adoption confidence scores. Exhibit 5-4
shows that "yes" respondents who saw the Monsanto presentation had lesser confidence drops in going from the original low-
risk to the subsequent high-risk decisions than did Denver or
Anonymous viewers in only 7 of 12 comparisons. That is, under high-risk (adoption) conditions, Monsanto "yes" confidences tended to hold up better, but only slightly so.

When the confidence scores for adoption decisions are broken down by affirmative-vs.-negative responses, as in both Exhibits 5-1 and 5-2, it is clear that there is no clear-cut source
effect for "yes" answers under these high-risk conditions. But
for "no" answers there is a source effect in favor of Monsanto.
In 9 of 12 comparisons in Exhibit 5-2 Monsanto's confidence
scores on "no" answers are higher than for Denver or Anonymous, for a 7.3% significance level. In view of abundant earlier evidence (Chapter 4) of a source effect in favor of Monsanto on simple tabulations of "yes"-vs.-"no" answers, these
greater confidence scores for Monsanto "no" answers suggest
one highly probable conclusion: the "no" answers are an effect,
not a cause, of the higher confidence scores. The respondent
seems to have to have greater confidence in his response in
order to say "no" to a well-known company than to a less well-

known or anonymous company. Thus a well-known company is better insulated not only against the probability of negative responses, but also against counterpersuasion on affirmative responses. This is particularly true of chemists and students as compared to purchasing agents. Thus, as with the raw yes-no answers to the adoption-vs.-referral questions (Chapter 4), in the confidence scores associated with their answers purchasing agents were least affected by company reputation.

Exhibit 5-2 also shows that purchasing agents had a different pattern of confidence scores as between good-vs.-poor presentations. While the "yes" adoption confidence scores of chemists and students were generally higher in the poor than in the good presentations, in the case of purchasing agents the good presentations had higher confidence scores. As pointed out in Chapter 4, purchasing agents not only acted favorably on a fewer proportion of both good and poor adoption presentations; they also much more deeply reduced their proportion of affirmative answers in going from good to poor presentations than the other groups, particularly chemists. Thus the reduction of the already low proportion of their affirmative answers in going from good to poor presentations was matched *pari passu* by a reduction in their confidence scores. Hence while purchasing agent choices were more adversely affected by poor presentation and less favorably affected by good presentation than were chemist choices, on the fewer good presentations that the former accepted they were more confident than chemists about these choices, and on the poor-presentation choices they accepted they were less confident.

All this suggests that when it came to the influence of the source, purchasing agents were more objective (perhaps more rational) buyers than chemists, but they were less objective when it came to the influence of the presentation quality. All audiences were always more secure in saying "no" than "yes," regardless of the presentation, but purchasing agents were less secure in saying "yes" to a poor presentation than chemists.

EXHIBIT 5-5

RESPONDENT SELF-CONFIDENCE SCORES: Negative Responses to
Adoption Questions, by Audience, and by Poor Monsanto
vs. Good Denver and Good Anonymous Presentations *

Audience	Monsanto Poor	Denver Good	Anonymous Good
Purchasing Agents	7.6	7.5	8.4
Chemists	7.3	7.0	6.3
Students	6.8	5.8	5.1

* This table consists of those respondents who said "yes," they would
refer and then shifted to "no," they would not adopt. The confidence scores
are based on the adoption responses.

This indicates that purchasing agents particularly are harder
to convince that a change from the present product should be
made in the first place; and, having decided on the strength
of a poor presentation to make a change, they are easier to
convince that they ought to return to the original product.
That is, once they have made a change on the strength of a
poor presentation they are, more than the chemists who were
subject to the presentation, susceptible to counterpersuasion.

The relative influence of the source vs. the presentation as
between purchasing agents on the one hand and chemists and
students on the other is shown in Exhibit 5-5. This exhibit
gives the adoption confidence scores for the three groups as
between a poor Monsanto and good Denver and good Anonymous presentations for all respondents who said "yes," they
would refer the product onward, but "no," they would not
adopt it directly themselves. It will be recalled from Chapter 4
(especially Exhibit 4-6) that chemists and students were more
susceptible to source effect than purchasing agents. Now Exhibit 5-5 shows that unlike purchasing agents, chemists and
students also had much greater confidences in their "no's" for
a poor Monsanto presentation than for good Denver and good
Anonymous presentations. Since such a high Monsanto source
effect among chemists and students has already been demon-

strated, these results suggest that "confidence" should be viewed as both an antecedent and a consequence, depending on the situation. Thus chemists and students were so powerfully influenced in favor of the Monsanto source that when this well-known source made a poor presentation they were forced to be particularly sure of themselves before rejecting it. In one case the source *produces* confidence and in another it *requires* confidence to resist or reject the source.

All this helps to demonstrate the by-now obvious fact that generalizations about industrial purchasing behavior are treacherous unless one distinguishes between specifically who the purchasers are and specifically what decisions they are asked to make.

Self-confidence and decision risks: Follow-up responses

As noted earlier, communications researchers have repeatedly verified the existence of a sleeper effect: the tendency of source effect influences to diminish with the passage of time such that the opinions of persons subjected to identical or similar messages from different sources tend to become more similar as time passes.

The present research tested the effect of time only with respect to respondents' referral (low-risk) decisions and their self-confidence on these decisions. As pointed out in Chapter 4, there was a sleeper effect, both regarding source and presentation, and it affected different audiences somewhat differently. The following analysis shows that it is not only respondents' actions that change over time (based on a five-week follow-up questionnaire), but also the degree of confidence they have in their actions.

Exhibit 5-6 produces some startlingly clear results. Persons who said "yes" on the original referral question as well as "yes" on the referral follow-up (Columns 2 and 4) always had *lower* consolidated confidence scores on their follow-up than on their original responses, and persons who said "yes"

EXHIBIT 5-6

REFERRAL SELF-CONFIDENCE SCORES: Original and Follow-up, by Types and Conditions of Responses

Referral Question	*Types and Conditions of Responses* *					
	Y/Y/Y	Y/Y/N	Y/N/Y	Y/N/N	N/N/Y	N/N/N
(1)	(2)	(3)	(4)	(5)	(6)	(7)
Original	7.5	7.8	7.1	5.9	7.3	7.1
Follow-up	7.2	8.8	6.4	6.4	7.3	7.9

* The letters (Y and N) in Columns 2 through 7 refer to the Y = "yes" and N = "no" answers which respondents gave to three questions in sequence, namely 1/2/3. Thus in Column 3, Y/Y/N means that the respondent said:

1. "Yes" to the original referral question;
2. "Yes" to the original adoption question;
3. "No" to the follow-up referral question;

and that on the original referral question his confidence score was 7.8 and on the follow-up, 8.8.

on the original and "no" on the follow-up (Columns 3 and 5) always had *higher* consolidated follow-up confidence scores. Indeed, in each cell in Exhibit 5-6 the follow-up "no's" always had higher confidences than the original questions, regardless of the original responses, and in the only case where a follow-up "yes" score was not lower than the original score (Column 6), it was unchanged.

According to Student's *t* test, the probabilities that there is a significant difference between the results in each column of Exhibit 5-6 are as follows:

Col. 2–70%
3–90%
4–70%
5–80%
6–no difference
7–99%

This confirms the risk-reduction hypotheses of consumer behavior: follow-up confidence drops for "yes" respondents and rises for "no" respondents. Persons feel more secure with "no" than with "yes" answers on the follow-up, just as they did in their original answers, even when their total risk (responsibility) is minimal.

Examination of these results for the influence of source and presentation effects reveals some differences. This is done in Exhibit 5-7, but for "yes/yes/yes" and "yes/no/yes" answers

EXHIBIT 5-7

SELF-CONFIDENCE SCORES, ORIGINAL VS. FOLLOW-UP: Difference in Referral Scores, by Types and Conditions of Responses, and Source and Quality of Presentation

	Original Minus Follow-up Scores, by Types and Conditions of Responses *					
	Yes/Yes/Yes			*Yes/No/Yes*		
Quality of Presentation	*Monsanto*	*Denver*	*Anonymous*	*Monsanto*	*Denver*	*Anonymous*
Good	(0.23)	(0.52)	(0.24)	(0.03)	(0.48)	(0.63)
Poor	0.10	0.14	0.10	(0.04)	0.41	(0.72)

* See the note to Exhibit 5-6 for explanation of "Yes/Yes/Yes" and "Yes/No/Yes." Parentheses designate negative numbers, which indicate higher follow-up scores.

only, owing to the small sample sizes of the other responses. For each type of presentation (good and poor), the exhibit shows the results of subtracting follow-up referral confidence scores from original referral confidence scores. A negative number indicates a higher follow-up score and a positive number, a lower follow-up score. Thus people who saw the good presentation always had a follow-up confidence rise (negative number), while those who saw the poor presentation generally had a follow-up drop. The higher level of good-presentation scores after five weeks is significant at the 1.56% level according to the binomial test and the lower poor-presentation pattern of results is significant at the 34.4% level. Hence there appears to be a positive sleeper effect associated with presentation quality. The confidence-producing effect of a good presentation accelerates over time, as does the confidence-detracting effect of a less-good (poor) presentation. The advantages of a good sales presentation over a poor one tend to expand and become strengthened with the passage of time. Hence sleeper effect works "against" a high-credibility source but "for" a well-presented message.

Regarding source effect, Exhibit 5-7 shows no significant pattern of confidence changes between Monsanto and Denver and Anonymous for the poor presentation, and for the good presentation, while there are some apparent patterns, they are weak and inconclusive. It can therefore be said that a sleeper effect apparently works on the confidence that respondents have in their answers, but that this effect is more clearly related to presentation than to source.

The above findings extend the concept of sleeper effect beyond its previous applications in several respects:

1. Previously, sleeper effect has always been associated with source credibility. The present findings indicate that it also applies to the message.

2. Previous research has always indicated that sleeper effect is a negative phenomenon. The present research shows that it can also consist of an enhanced effect. It can, for example, enhance the power of a well-presented message.

3. Previously, only opinions, attitudes, and information-retention have been labeled as being subject to sleeper effect. The present findings add the confidence which the audience has in its responses to messages.

OTHER DECISION INFLUENCES: SELLER'S PRODUCT CLAIMS, SALESMAN'S PRODUCT KNOWLEDGE AND TRUSTWORTHINESS, AND BUYER'S INFORMATION RETENTION

It is universally accepted that every communication communicates more things than it intends, and that some of the things it intends to communicate frequently do not get communicated. The things that are unintentionally communicated may be just as powerful as the intentional things, and the intended things that do not get communicated can cripple the communicator's effectiveness.

In the present research an effort was made to examine these phenomena. One of the unintentional communications that is likely to affect an audience's attitudes and decisions is source trustworthiness—the trustworthiness of the message source (the company which sponsors the message) and the trustworthiness of the message communicator (the salesman who transmits the message). Hovland, Weiss, Kelman, and others have shown that source effect is basically a function of the perceived trustworthiness of the source. What is not entirely clear from their work is the exact identity of the source: is it the message communicator, or is it the group, organization, nation, company, or professional discipline he represents? Thus in the Kelman-Hovland research on opinion change regarding juvenile delinquency issues,[6] there is no way of knowing exactly what made the judge, who was classified as a "positive" and high-trust source, more trustworthy than the thug, who was classified as a "negative" and low-trust source. To what extent was the positive source more credible because he was a judge, or because he was a recognized expert on juvenile problems aside from being a judge, or because of his pronunciation, voice, and style of delivering his message?

Clearly differences in the wording and the delivery of a message can make a difference in the resulting audience behavior. The Kelman-Hovland juvenile delinquency experiment, which was specifically designed to test source effect, held the wording of the actual message absolutely constant, as well as attempting to hold as constant as possible all other variables. But the powerful influence of presentation which the present

---

[6] Herbert C. Kelman and Carl I. Hovland, " 'Reinstatement' of the Communicator in Delayed Measurement of Opinion Change," 1953.

research has encountered suggests that the Kelman-Hovland results should be more carefully examined to determine whether a presentation effect might have been present in what was assumed to be an experiment that varied only the source.

Such a possibility seems clearly to exist. In their experiment one message transmitter (the judge) was introduced to the audience, according to the experimenters, to give "the impression of being a sincere, honest, and public-spirited individual, with a great deal of warmth and understanding for juvenile delinquents," [7] while the other message transmitter (the thug) was introduced to give "the impression of being an obnoxious, self-centered individual with a shady past and present . . . [who] showed disrespect of the law and the community . . . [and whose] advocacy of lenient [juvenile delinquency] treatment was [clearly] motivated by self-interest and disrespect for law." [8] Then, according to the authors, each experimental group separately listened to a message on juvenile delinquency from one of these clearly identified sources, the message being "identical in wording." Hence only the source was presumed to have varied. However, the authors go on to say that for each message transmitter, "Differences in voice and style of delivery were introduced in keeping with the personalities suggested by the introductions." [9] Obviously, even though the content and wording of the intended "central" message remained identical as between the different sources, the unintended "peripheral" message varied as between the sources. In an effort to make each source's message consistent with the source's personal background and interests—that is, in order to make the whole experimental situation realistic and therefore believable for its subjects—the authors varied the presentation. The warmhearted judge was made to sound like a warmhearted

[7] *Ibid.*, p. 329.
[8] *Ibid.*, pp. 329–330.
[9] *Ibid.*, p. 330.

judge, and the cynical thug was made to sound like a cynical thug, even though both literally spoke the identical words.

The present research has demonstrated that when both the words and their delivery are varied, a powerful presentation effect shows up. In view of this strong result, it seems reasonable to suppose that when just one of these variables, such as delivery (voice and style), is varied, it can by itself have its own autonomous effect. Kelman and Hovland obviously varied one variable—the delivery. But their study does not indicate whether or how this might have affected their results. Nor does it clearly indicate an awareness of the possibility that "delivery" (presentation) is a possible influence or issue. Because of this, serious questions arise about exactly what this experiment measured. To be sure, there is a great body of research results supporting the existence of source effect, including the present study. But only the present study has been specifically designed to measure the effect of presentation in the context of measuring source effect. And the present study's results seem to suggest that there may be more to "source effect" than meets the eye, without in any way impugning source effect as a powerful factor in itself.

It might be argued, of course, that the alteration of the communicators' voices and styles in the Kelman-Hovland experiment merely reinforced the respective identities of the sources (that is, their respective trustworthiness and credibility), and that therefore these factors were not the contaminating independent variables the present research suggests they were. But in view of the present research's findings of a strong presentation effect, one would hesitate to accept such an argument. The extent to which one might be willing to accept it is easily seen by one's answer to the following question: If you had a choice of experimental designs with which to test the Kelman-Hovland statement that their measured differences in opinion change as between the judge's audiences and the thug's audi-

ences were entirely a matter of source effect, which of the
following designs would you select?

1. The design they employed, which varied each communicator's "voice and style of delivery."
2. Or a design which would not have varied his voice and
   style of delivery.

It is unlikely that a single reader would choose design "1."
On the other hand, it is important to recognize that the existence of source effect is not really in doubt. A variety of
researches which were not disabled by the suggested contami-
nation in Kelman-Hovland have clearly proved it. Indeed,
Hovland himself has proved it in other studies in which everything about the message and its presentation was held constant.[10] However, as noted in Chapter 4, since competing communicators never have either identical messages ("words") or
identical presentations ("voices and styles") in any realistic
situation, it seems reasonable to face the issue of how much
the differences in words and voices and styles affect the so-
called source effect. For example, does a good presentation by
a low-credibility source carry more weight than a poor presentation by a high-credibility source? What is the relative importance of the words in a presentation versus the voice and the
style?

If there is to be any meaningful application of communications research findings to real-world situations, such questions
must be faced. And indeed Kelman and Hovland clearly sought
to avoid undue abstraction in their research by designing their
presentation such that "Differences in voice and style of delivery were introduced in keeping with the personalities suggested
by the introductions . . . [of the message transmitters]." In
other words, Kelman and Hovland wanted to be as realistic as
possible under the circumstances and took steps in that direc-

---

[10] Most specifically in Carl I. Hovland and Walter Weiss, "The Influence of Source Credibility on Communications Effectiveness," 1952.

tion. It is now necessary to take even more steps in that direction.

The question that needs answering deals with the relative influence of the real source of the message (the company) vs. that of, as it were, the source's ventriloquist, namely the message transmitter (the salesman), vs. that of the message itself. Exhibit 5-8 helps provide an answer. It shows the results of

EXHIBIT 5-8

RELIABILITY OF SOURCES' PRODUCT CLAIMS: Adopting Respondents' Average Ratings of Reliability of Company's Over-All Product Claims, by Respondents' Decisions and by Source and Quality of Sales Presentations *

Respondent Answer to Adoption Question	Good Presentation			Poor Presentation		
	Mon-santo	Den-ver	Anony-mous	Mon-santo	Den-ver	Anony-mous
Yes	7.4	6.9	7.0	6.8	6.0	6.8
No	7.2	6.1	6.7	6.9	5.6	5.0
Total	7.3	6.5	6.8	6.8	5.7	5.8

* The ratings are based on a 9-point scale. The higher the rating, the higher the perceived reliability.

respondents' reliability ratings of the product claims of the company (message source), divided according to the quality of the salesman's (transmitter's) presentation. The specific question put to the subjects was:

"We tend to have different feelings about the product claims made by various companies. Considering everything, what do you think about the product claims of the company the sales engineer represented—not just about the claims for this one particular product, but about the company's product claims generally? Please rank on the following scale your feelings about *this* company's over-all product claims."

Very unreliable		Very reliable

In coding the responses, blocks were numbered 1 through 9 from left to right. The more reliable the claims were thought to be, the higher the ratings.

What this question in effect does is measure source credibility in a relatively clean way rather than merely reflecting it in an ambiguous way, as previous tabulations have in part done. The reason it is a distinct *measure* is that by asking respondents to *rate* the product claims of different companies making identical presentations (three sets of identical "good" and three sets of identical "poor" presentations), the differences between the sources' resulting composite ratings for any one quality of presentation can really reflect only one possible controlled variable: the perceived reliabilities of the source companies. The differences between reliability ratings of companies which, in the eyes of the raters, are distinguished by nothing but their names, must, *pari passu,* measure differences in the perceived reliabilities of these companies and nothing else, other than the usual experimental "noise." Given the homogeneity of each responding cell, what is yielded is a relatively clean measure of source effect in an experimental situation that has come closer to simulating reality than any known experimental research on source effect. Yet to say this is actually to ignore the outcome of the ratings. The complete elimination of all outside influences, leaving only source effect to show up, requires that the differences between the Monsanto ratings for each decision and their equivalent Denver and Anonymous decision ratings be equal as between good presentations and poor presentations. Thus if on a "yes" response to a good presentation the difference between Monsanto and Denver is —0.5 (which it is in Exhibit 5-8), then it should be the same for the poor presentation. The fact is that it is not. The experiment is not absolutely clean. Other factors are operating. The most obvious one is the composition of the audiences in each cell. The audience composition in each cell is similar, but each is composed of three different groups, and in each case in slightly different proportions. This will be examined more closely later.

For the moment, however, Exhibit 5-8 does show that there has been a true source effect. For both "yes" and "no" answers, and for both "good" and "poor" presentations, Monsanto rates as high as or higher than either Denver or Anonymous in 11 out of 12 comparisons. This means that there is only a 0.32% probability that the Monsanto ratings are equal to the Denver and Anonymous ratings. The actual source-effect coefficient is the average weighted difference between the two Monsanto ratings and the four competing company ratings, or about 0.95 confidence points.[11]

Exhibit 5-8 actually shows source effect in two ways: one by the differences between the Monsanto ratings and the Denver and Anonymous ratings, and two by the differences between the "yes" and the "no" ratings. It will be noted that five out of six "yes" product-reliability claims ratings are higher than the "no" ratings. And in the one exception there is a virtual tie—6.8 vs. 6.9. Since a higher rating indicates greater confidence in the source, and since five-sixths of these greater-confidence ratings were associated with favorable adoption decisions, this means that the power of source credibility is confirmed in a second way, both based on a measure of source trustworthiness. Credibility is clearly related to trustworthiness, which confirms the Hovland-Weiss finding that high-credibility sources received significantly higher "trustworthiness" ratings than low-credibility sources.[12] The higher the source credibility, the lower the dissonance in the respondent's reactions.

A definite presentation effect is also apparent. In every comparison good-presentation ratings are higher than poor-presentation ratings. Generally speaking, these results suggest that it

---

[11] Exhibit 5-8 also shows that there is a message effect on the source. Companies are rated higher after the good than after the poor presentation.

[12] "The Influence of Source Credibility . . . ," *loc. cit.*

is probably more effective for an industrial products producer to build a reputation for quality products via good sales presentations than via advertising and public relations. But, as noted before, "presentations" are a combination of many things which should interest the communicator; e.g., the actual words he uses and their arrangement, the appearance, manner, voice, and style of the salesman, and so forth.

Just as Exhibit 5-8 tries to clarify what a "clean" source effect is, so it is necessary to examine presentation effect by looking at its various components and their impacts. Exhibit 5-9 looks at some of these components. It is based on the following question, which was the last question asked in the "opinion" and "action" section of the first questionnaire:

> "When one listens to a sales presentation, one develops various degrees of trust in the salesman. How would you rate the trustworthiness of the salesman in the film? (Please check one block)."

| Very
untrustworthy | | | | | | | | | Very
trustworthy |

Exhibit 5-9 shows that for both "yes" and "no" answers the salesman received a much higher trustworthiness rating when he made a good presentation than when he made a poor one. It also shows that the trust ratings of the respondents who adopted the product ("yes" answers) were always higher than of those who rejected it ("no" answers). Thus trust in the salesman has a great deal to do with adoption, and the quality of his presentation has a great deal to do with how trustworthy customers rate him as being. It is unfortunately impossible to analyze Exhibit 5-9 in any way that explains how much each of the various major presentation components contributes toward presentation "quality"; i.e., how much it is the words and arrangements of words used in the body of the message, how much it is the message transmitter's voice, style, manner, and

EXHIBIT 5-9

SALESMAN'S TRUSTWORTHINESS: Adopting Respondents' Average
Trustworthiness Ratings of the Salesman, by Respondents' Decisions and by Source and Quality of Sales Presentation *

Respondent Answer to Adoption Question	Good Presentation			Poor Presentation		
	Mon-santo	Den-ver	Anony-mous	Mon-santo	Den-ver	Anony-mous
Yes	7.2	7.4	7.0	4.9	5.9	6.5
No	6.5	6.2	6.3	4.5	4.8	5.0
Total	6.9	6.8	6.6	4.6	5.0	5.4

* The ratings are based on a 9-point scale. The higher the rating the
higher the trust.

so forth. But that the latter are operative in a powerful way is
suggested by the differences between the ratings in Exhibits
5-8 and 5-9. Setting these ratings next to each other is exceedingly revealing:

	Good Presentation			Poor Presentation		
"Yes" Answers	M	D	A	M	D	A
Company trust	7.4	6.9	7.0	6.8	6.0	6.8
Salesman trust	7.2	7.4	7.0	4.9	5.9	6.5
"No" Answers						
Company trust	7.2	6.1	6.7	6.9	5.6	5.0
Salesman trust	6.5	6.2	6.3	4.5	4.8	5.4

Assume each set of matched trust ratings (a company rating and a salesman rating) is a single response cell. The tabulation shows that in only one of the twelve cells are the company and the salesman ratings identical. In all others they are
different. In the case of the good presentation, these differences are sometimes negligible but never is there a clear-cut
pattern of one scoring higher or lower—that is, the company
or the salesman. But in the poor presentation there is a clear
pattern. Five times out of six the company trust score is higher
than the salesman trust score, and it tends to be higher by a

relatively wide margin. If presentation consisted only of the
content and wording of the intended message, one would expect all the differences between matched source and matched
salesman ratings to be identical. Thus, in the above tabulation
among "yes" answers, one would expect the difference between the Monsanto company trust and the Monsanto salesman trust ($7.4 - 7.2 = 0.2$) to be identical with the matched
cell of respondents exposed to the poor presentations ($6.8 -
4.9 = 1.9$). But the differences are not identical. Some other
factor has crept in. The extent to which it has crept in can be
seen by averaging the differences between the above good and
poor presentations. The following tabulation shows the average differences between these good and poor presentations, by
company trust rating and by salesman trust rating. That is, the
average poor-presentation rating has in each case been sub-
tracted from the average good-presentation rating. The results show the extent to which the average poor rating is lower
than the average good one.

	Monsanto	Denver	Anonymous
Company trust	0.5	0.8	1.0
Salesman trust	2.3	1.8	1.2

These differences seem to lead to only one conclusion—
what is communicated about trust in identical presentations
varies as between whose trustworthiness is involved. When the
questions involved the salesman's company, the good presentation did indeed make the company seem more trustworthy
than the poor one. But when the trustworthiness of the salesman himself was up for judgment, the effect of the differences
between the two presentations was very considerable. The
poor presentation produced a virtual collapse in the respondents' trust of the salesman. The explanation seems to be that
when respondents were asked to rate the trustworthiness of the
salesman they became much more conscious of the salesman

and everything he did in the presentation than when they were merely asked to rate the company he represented. Since respondents have already been shown to have had a definite source-effect "bias," the presumption is that the "bias" against the salesman (as opposed to the company) which so clearly shows up in the above tabulation must have crept into all the preceding tabulations which showed a presentation effect. Clearly the personality and the "voice and style of delivery" of the source's message transmitter have a powerful and autonomous presentation effect.

The existence of differences in audience reactions as between salesmen and the companies they represent has also been demonstrated by Bauer.[13] In his study of drug adoption by physicians, he found that with relatively low-risk drugs the correlation of drug preference with salesman and company preference was about equal. However, with risky drugs, preference for the company was about twice as strong as preference for the salesman. In other words, the salesman was perceived as a less reliable source, and therefore a more risky source, than his company. To the extent that this is true, it would seem reasonable that the manner and quality of the salesman's presentation become particularly important factors in determining the extent of the customer's faith in him. The greater the risk the more reassurance the customer requires. If he can be reassured by the salesman as well as his company, that much the better. Hence the customer can be expected to "look for" reassurance. One thing the salesman can provide is the manner and quality of his presentation. Hence presentation effect is an element of audience decision making.

The tabulation also suggests the existence of a powerful "negative" source effect. Thus not only is there a greater difference among salesmen than among companies in the extent to which their respective poor presentations rank below their

---

[13] Raymond A. Bauer, "Risk Handling in Drug Adoption: The Role of Company Preference," 1961.

good presentations, but there is also an interesting difference in the way this shows up between specific companies. For example, the poor-presentation average salesman trust rating is 2.3 units below the good-presentation rating in the case of Monsanto, 1.8 in the case of Denver, and 1.2 in the case of Anonymous. In the case of company trust ratings, the *direction* of the difference is exactly the opposite: Monsanto 0.5, Denver 0.8, Anonymous 1.0.

In other words, the usual source effect pattern shows up when we compare company trust ratings. But when we compare salesman trust ratings, the pattern is almost the direct opposite—the higher the company credibility, the lower is the salesman's trustworthiness. The pattern is clearly evident in the poor presentation, as shown in Exhibit 5-9.

All this supports in still another way the point made earlier in this chapter that source effect may be a double-edged sword capable of striking in opposite directions. The higher a company's trustworthiness (credibility), apparently the higher are its audience's expectations. Since the audience therefore has higher standards for a favorably well-known company's representative than for representatives of companies it does not know, it will rate the known company's salesman lower. (See Chapter 6 for confirmation of this finding on still other grounds, but for an alternative interpretation of its meaning.) Thus there is a reverse source effect. It imposes on the high-credibility company the special obligation of making special efforts to upgrade and sustain a special high level of performance by its salesmen.

Finally, these differences between company trustworthiness and salesman trustworthiness show once again the necessity for greater precision in discussions about source effect. In the present research, the source of the spoken sales message was the salesman, and the source of the salesman was his company. When we talk of "source effect," whom do we have in mind, the company or the salesman? As noted above, if we have the company in mind, the present research confirms the Hovland-Weiss finding that the high-credibility source receives a significantly higher trustworthiness rating than the low-credibility source. But if we have the salesman in mind and rate *his* trustworthiness, the present research in part contradicts Hovland and Weiss—in the case of the poor presentation, a salesman from the high-credibility company source who does a poor job apparently gets a significantly lower trust rating than an equally inept salesman from the low-credibility company source.

As noted earlier in this chapter and in Chapter 4, different audiences seem to react differently to different stimuli. A breakdown of the company-trust results of Exhibit 5-8 to show how our three different audiences voted is therefore desirable. This is done in Exhibit 5-10.

EXHIBIT 5-10

RELIABILITY OF SELLER'S PRODUCT CLAIMS: Adopting Respondents' Reliability Ratings of Company's Over-All Product Claims, by Respondent Categories, by Respondents' Decisions, and by Source and Quality of Sales Presentation *

Respondent Category and Answer to Adoption Question		Good Presentation			Poor Presentation		
		Mon-santo	Den-ver	Anony-mous	Mon-santo	Den-ver	Anony-mous
(1)		(2)	(3)	(4)	(5)	(6)	(7)
Purchasing							
Agents	Yes	7.9	7.0	7.7	6.5	5.7	6.0
	No	7.5	6.5	7.5	6.8	5.8	6.0
Chemists	Yes	7.4	7.3	7.6	7.3	6.7	7.0
	No	7.2	6.2	6.3	7.1	5.6	5.8
Students	Yes	7.3	6.6	6.5	6.2	5.7	7.0
	No	6.7	5.7	6.1	6.7	5.4	5.0

* The ratings are based on a 9-point scale. The higher the rating, the higher the perceived reliability.

EXHIBIT 5-11

SALESMAN'S TRUSTWORTHINESS: Adopting Respondents' Average
Trustworthiness Ratings of the Salesman, by Respondent
Categories, by Respondents' Decisions, and by Source
and Quality of Sales Presentation *

Respondent Category and Answer to Adoption Question		Good Presentation			Poor Presentation		
		Mon-santo	Den-ver	Anony-mous	Mon-santo	Den-ver	Anony-mous
(1)		(2)	(3)	(4)	(5)	(6)	(7)
Purchasing Agents	Yes	8.0	7.2	8.5	5.0	6.7	8.5
	No	6.9	7.3	8.1	6.1	5.6	6.0
Chemists	Yes	7.3	8.4	7.0	4.7	5.3	6.5
	No	6.4	6.3	5.4	3.9	4.2	5.3
Students	Yes	6.8	7.0	6.3	5.0	5.7	5.8
	No	6.1	5.1	6.1	3.5	4.6	4.3

* The ratings are based on a 9-point scale. The higher the rating, the
higher the trust.

Exhibit 5-11 does the same thing for the salesman trust
tabulations of Exhibit 5-9. Perhaps the most interesting result
of comparing Exhibits 5-10 and 5-11 is to see the enormous
extent to which chemists are influenced by source effect—the
extent to which they perceive a poor presentation as being in
some special way the fault of the message transmitter, not the
company he represents. While the salesman should, of course,
be blamed for a poor presentation, in the present case it appears that chemists actually overprotect the company and un-
derblame the man. This can be seen by comparing the differences between the trust ratings chemists give to poor and to
good presentations. In rating companies (Exhibit 5-10) their
poor-presentation scores are very close to their good-presentation scores. With all the former scores below the latter, the
differences are as follows:

	Company Ratings		
	M	D	A
Yes	0.1 *	0.6	0.6
No	0.1	0.6	0.5

* This means that the average "good" score of chemists who adopted the product and saw the Monsanto presentation was 0.1 points above the average "poor" score of chemists who adopted the product and saw the Monsanto presentation.

But in rating salesmen, here are the differences figured in the same way:

	Salesman Ratings		
	M	D	A
Yes	2.6	3.1	0.5
No	2.5	2.1	0.1

As Exhibits 5-10 and 5-11 both show, the average good-presentation rating levels in both exhibits are about the same. The extraordinary differences shown above result almost entirely from the great drop in the chemists' poor-presentation ratings of the salesmen. Purchasing agents were not nearly as hard on the salesmen, as the following tabulations show:

	Company Ratings		
	M	D	A
Yes	1.4 *	1.3	1.7
No	0.7	0.7	1.5

	Salesman Ratings		
	M	D	A
Yes	3.0	0.5	0.0
No	0.8	1.7	2.1

* This means that the average "good" score of purchasing agents who adopted the product and saw the Monsanto presentation was 1.4 points above the average "poor" score of purchasing agents who adopted the product and saw the Monsanto presentation.

It was seen earlier in this chapter, and in Chapter 4, that chemists were especially influenced by source effect, tending strongly to favor the well-known company. The above suggests that on top of this they trust a company more than its sales representative, and that when a sales presentation is poor they blame not the source (the company) but its transmitter (the salesman).

Indeed the chemists' reactions on this score are merely an exaggerated version of other respondents' reactions. Thus each audience category's average salesman's trust rating on poor presentations tends to be lower than its equivalent company rating. That is, the raw scores in the right panel of Exhibit 5-11 are lower, and often substantially lower, than those in the right panel of Exhibit 5-10. This strongly suggests that "presentation" may be more than merely a matter of the words that are used. The presenter's personality and manner and voice almost certainly enter in, and there seems to be a clear possibility that they may well affect some audiences more than others.

This therefore strongly suggests one other point: it is probably no more accurate to speak of "presentation effect" or "audience effect" as if they were clearly unidimensional in character than it is to speak of "source effect" in this way. It is clear that the "source" whose effectiveness is being alluded to probably consists of many things. In the present case, it almost certainly consists not just of the company which sells the product but also of the salesman through whom it delivers its sales message. The obvious differences with which different "deliverers" are perceived and the obvious differences with which they are perceived by different audiences—these facts require extreme caution in generalizing about source effect phenomena. Thus in the Kelman-Hovland research, though conducted with utmost care and precision, it is still not clear what "source" really influenced the audience: the speaker in his capacity as a judge, as a criminologist, as a gentle humanitarian, or as a soft-voiced human being, or perhaps it was not

EXHIBIT 5-12

SALESMAN'S KNOWLEDGE OF PRODUCT: Respondents' Ratings of
Salesman's Product Knowledge, by Respondents' Categories
and Adoption Decisions, and by Source and Quality
of Sales Presentation *

Respondent Category and Answer to Adoption Question		Good Presentation			Poor Presentation		
		Mon-santo	*Den-ver*	*Anony-mous*	*Mon-santo*	*Den-ver*	*Anony-mous*
Purchasing Agents	Yes	7.9	8.1	9.0	5.5	8.3	8.0
	No	7.9	7.4	8.6	6.4	6.8	6.4
Chemists	Yes	7.4	8.4	8.3	5.7	7.3	6.0
	No	7.0	7.1	7.2	4.7	5.7	5.1
Students	Yes	7.9	7.7	7.5	7.2	7.7	6.8
	No	7.3	7.3	8.1	3.9	6.1	6.0

* The ratings are based on a 9-point scale. The higher the respondents'
estimate of the salesman's product knowledge, the higher the ratings.

the speaker at all but rather the legal profession, the profession
of criminologists, or the voice as Christian charity.

It has now been shown that there is some relationship between audience action and its trust in the message source,
whether the latter is the sponsoring company and/or its trans-
mitting agent (salesman). It has also been suggested that trust
in the salesman is a function of many things. Exhibit 5-12
looks at one of these: the respondents' estimates of the salesman's knowledge of the product he is selling. The specific question asked was:

"Salesmen vary in the degree of their knowledge of the products they sell. Please indicate your estimate of the salesman's
knowledge of the product in the film you saw. (Please check
one block.)"

| Very unknowl-edgeable | | Very knowledge-able |

The results of this question (tabulated in Exhibit 5-12) are useful primarily in comparison with the information in Exhibit 5-11 on salesman trustworthiness. There are some interesting similarities and some surprising differences. The trust and knowledge results are similar in that:

1. The poor-presentation ratings are generally lower than the good-presentation ratings.
2. "Yes" ratings are generally higher than "no" ratings.
3. Trust and knowledge ratings generally move parallel to each other—they generally move in the same directions.

The differences in the results as between these two exhibits are considerably more revealing. Exhibit 5-13 tabulates these differences for each rating, subtracting in each case the "trust" rating from the "knowledge" rating. Thus a positive number indicates that the salesman's "knowledge" rating is higher than his "trust" rating, and a negative number indicates the reverse. The results are clear enough:

1. Knowledge is almost always rated higher than trust.
2. Relative to their judgments about the extent of the salesman's product knowledge, students are the least trusting of the salesmen.
3. Trust and knowledge ratings generally move parallel to each other—they generally move in the same directions.

These comparisons again confirm the existence of the frequently noted presentation effect. In doing so, however, they reveal something about the extent to which "presentation" measures the effect of personality, voice, and style, and not just the effect of the words, or of the script, used by the message transmitter.

The fact that all three audiences always rated the salesman's product knowledge higher than they rated his trustworthiness suggests that their reactions to him, and therefore their product adoption decisions, were influenced by the salesman in a way other than by what he specifically said about the prod-

EXHIBIT 5-13

COMPARISON OF SALESMAN'S KNOWLEDGE AND TRUST RATINGS:
Respondents' Ratings of Salesman's Product Knowledge Minus
Their Ratings of Salesman's Trustworthiness, by Respondents'
Categories and Adoption Decisions, and by Source and
Quality of Sales Presentation *

Respondent Category and Answer to Adoption Question		Good Presentation			Poor Presentation		
		Mon-santo	Den-ver	Anony-mous	Mon-santo	Den-ver	Anony-mous
Purchasing Agents	Yes	(0.1)	0.9	0.5	0.5	1.6	(0.5)
	No	1.0	0.1	0.5	0.3	1.2	0.4
Chemists	Yes	0.1	0.0	1.3	1.0	2.0	(0.5)
	No	0.6	0.8	1.8	0.8	1.5	(0.2)
Students	Yes	1.1	0.7	1.1	2.2	2.0	1.0
	No	1.2	2.1	2.0	0.4	1.5	1.7

* Parentheses indicate negative number.

ucts, its uses, and its virtues. They were presumably influenced by more than his words. They were influenced by what Kelman and Hovland classified as "source effect" but which actually seems to have contained a large element of presentation effect, namely the salesman's "voice and style of delivery" and other distinguishing mannerisms.

These comparisons suggest several other conclusions:

1. Even though a given level of faith in a salesman's product knowledge is not enough to induce an equivalent level of faith (trust) in that salesman himself, the two variables are related. Both rise and fall together.

2. The good over-all presentation appears to reduce the difference between a respondent's faith in the salesman's product knowledge and his faith (trust) in the salesman. A poor over-all presentation appears to widen the difference.

3. Students are the most suspicious (or, at least, the least trusting) of the three audiences, and this showed up most on

the good presentations (see also Exhibit 5-11). Hence student reactions, as suggested on the basis of other measures presented earlier in this study, should be generalized to the entire population or to other populations only with great care.

The relationship between the respondent's judgment about the salesman's product knowledge and his willingness to adopt the product follows a pattern similar to that noted in connection with trust ratings. This is, of course, to be expected since trust and knowledge ratings moved in parallel. As pointed out before, Exhibit 5-12 shows that people rated the salesman's knowledge higher for "yes" answers than for "no" answers. This holds for 15 out of 18 comparisons, indicating an edge for the "yes" answers at the 0.4% significance level under the binomial test.

Monsanto salesmen were generally considered as less knowledgeable than the Denver or Anonymous salesmen. Yet it was shown in Chapter 4 that Monsanto, by whatever breakdown, generally had the largest proportion of adoptions. In other words, neither a lower salesman's product-knowledge rating nor a lower salesman's trust rating prevented the respondents from more frequently adopting the product of the high-credibility company which the salesman represented. This suggests that the sales-producing (or persuasive) power of a high-credibility source is enormous, and/or that (as noted earlier) there is a reverse source effect which causes respondents to downgrade representatives of well-known companies (sources) because they have higher levels of expectations regarding the performances of these representatives.

The plausibility of a negative source effect is suggested by the results tabulated in Exhibit 5-14. This exhibit gives the respondents' average correct scores on ten information questions they were asked in Part II of the questionnaire they were given immediately after they saw the movie. The good and the poor filmed sales presentations each contained all the informa-

EXHIBIT 5-14

AUDIENCE INFORMATION RETENTION SCORES: Respondents'
Information Retention Scores, by Respondents' Categories and Adoption Decisions, and by Source
and Quality of Sales Presentation *

Respondent Category and Answer to Adoption Question		*Good Presentation*			*Poor Presentation*		
		Mon-santo	*Den-ver*	*Anony-mous*	*Mon-santo*	*Den-ver*	*Anony-mous*
Purchasing Agents	Yes	4.1	4.0	4.3	3.0	3.7	4.5
	No	5.3	4.6	4.7	4.6	4.3	3.1
Chemists	Yes	7.2	6.6	6.7	5.8	3.0	6.0
	No	6.4	6.7	6.2	5.3	5.3	5.7
Students	Yes	5.7	6.4	5.6	4.4	6.3	4.5
	No	5.1	5.5	6.0	5.2	4.4	5.0

* Maximum score equals 10, minimum equals zero.

tion needed to answer the information questionnaire. It was
necessary to see the movie to assure 100% accuracy in answering the information questions, although several answers
might have been guessed with better than a 50–50 chance of
being right.

Perhaps the most important result of Exhibit 5-14 is that
there is no significant source effect for either "yes" or "no" answers. That is, the information absorbed by the audience was
about the same for high- as for low-credibility companies. This
confirms the findings of Hovland and Weiss.[14] Furthermore,
comparing Exhibit 5-14 with Exhibits 5-11 and 5-12, we see
that the respondents' ratings of the salesman's product knowledge or his trustworthiness were not at all related to how much
information the salesman succeeded in effectively communicating to the respondents. That is, the amount of information retained by the respondents seems to have had nothing to do

---

[14] "The Influence of Source Credibility. . . ,"

with how they rated the salesman's product knowledge or trustworthiness. Since, therefore, respondents retained about as much information from the high- as from the low-credibility company source, it cannot be said that their lower product-knowledge ratings of salesmen from the high-credibility company (Monsanto, Exhibit 5-12) was due to an information transmission failure. It is likely that it was due simply to the respondents having higher expectations of the representatives of a high-credibility source. And if that is true, it was not any extraordinary pulling power of the source effect that explains the higher ratio of adopters among the Monsanto film viewers in the face of the company's low salesman's product-knowledge rating. Rather it was that the respondents had higher expectations of the salesman from the high-credibility company. This produced what we have called a negative source effect. But while it affected the respondents' opinions, it did not apparently greatly alter their decisions. The low salesman trust ratings of high-credibility companies did not reduce the ratio of product adoptions.

Hence, one of the most important conclusions suggested by Exhibits 5-11 and 5-12 is that the existence of opinion differences within or between groups, and the production of opinion changes within people, may be little or no indication of the existence of action differences or action changes. Opinions neither measure nor necessarily parallel or predict actions.

Exhibit 5-14 also seems to suggest the unlikelihood that messages from high-prestige, highly trusted companies might actually be less efficient than messages from low-prestige, less-trusted companies.[15] The possibility that this might be so is suggested by the notion that if an audience has great faith in a given source it listens less carefully to its message, while if it has less faith in that source it listens quite carefully in order

---

[15] Such a possibility was suggested in one situation by Rarick, *op. cit.*, and by Hilibrand, *op. cit.*

to assure itself that it is making a "safe" (low-risk) choice. If audiences behaved this way, this would have meant that the listener's initial response to the high-prestige company's sales presentation would have been very favorable, but that later when he had to convince others in his company that the proposed change be made, the listener who heard the low-prestige company's presentation would be more effective in persuading his colleagues than the high-prestige company listener. The reason for this would be that the listener to the high-prestige source's message would have retained less solid information than the listener to the low-prestige source's message. Hence the former would have had less solid information to transmit to his colleagues. The existence of this kind of situation was not confirmed in the present research.

SLEEPER EFFECT DECISION INFLUENCES

As already noted, the present research requestioned all audiences five weeks after the original questioning, but only on their referral actions. A matter that is of considerable interest in this regard is the relationship between audience information retention and change in audience action after the passage of time. That is, does greater immediate retention of the information communicated by the salesman affect the extent to which respondent decisions made at that time are sustained or altered five weeks later? Exhibit 5-15 attempts to answer that question. The numbers in the body of the exhibit are the information retention scores based on questions asked immediately after respondents saw the filmed sales presentations. The scores in the horizontal "yes" line are for respondents who five weeks after they saw the original film answered "yes" to the follow-up question of whether they would now refer the product onward to others in their company. The "no" line scores are for respondents who said "no" to the same question. The retention scores are then divided in Columns 2, 3, and 4

EXHIBIT 5-15

SLEEPER EFFECT AND INFORMATION RETENTION: Information
Retention Scores and Action Decisions, by Referral
Decisions after Five-Week Interval *

Follow-up Referral Decision	Original Decisions, by Type of Required Action		
	Referral–Yes Adoption–Yes	Referral–Yes Adoption–No	Referral–No Adoption–No
(1)	(2)	(3)	(4)
Yes	5.5	5.3	5.0
No	4.7	5.0	4.7

* The maximum information retention score is 10. The scores are based
on a questionnaire administered immediately after the original showing of
the film.

by respondents with the indicated mix of answers to the referral
and adoption questions asked immediately after they saw the
film. Thus the 5.5 in Column 2 means that persons who originally said "yes," they would refer the product onward, and
also said "yes," they would adopt it, and who then five weeks
later also said "yes," they would refer it onward—their information retention score was 5.5. The exhibit shows that
people who answered "yes" in the five-week follow-up referral
question had, regardless of the mix of their original referral-
adoption answers, better information retention scores at the
time of the original sales presentation than those who answered "no" on the follow-up.

While the differences are small, the probabilities that the
differences between the "yes" and the "no" follow-up referral
scores are significant, according to Student's *t* test, are:

Yes/Yes = 90%
Yes/No = 60%
No/No = 40% (not significantly different)

By the binomial test the higher information retention scores
of the "yes" follow-up respondents over the "no" respondents

in three of three cases indicates that the information retention of the former was higher at the 12% significance level.

It can therefore be said that the sleeper effect tendency which was shown in Chapter 4 to reduce the power of the source effect is itself probably moderated as the amount of information originally retained by the audience increases. Thus the more effectively information is communicated to the audience at the time of the original communication, the less likely the audience is to change its decision with the passage of time.

CHAPTER 6

The Ingredients of Source, Presentation, and Audience Effects

THE ANALYSIS in Chapter 5 showed that while a communication can affect an audience's opinions and actions, the confidence the audience has in these opinions and actions can greatly influence their stability and duration. Moreover, it was shown that while source effect is present in industrial purchasing behavior, and while it varies as between both the type of industrial purchaser and the amount of personal risk to which a decision subjects him, the source can also affect the amount of self-confidence various types of purchasers can have in decisions involving various amounts of personal risk.

In addition it was pointed out that what has sometimes been defined as being a clean source effect may actually have included a good deal of presentation effect. This raises the further question of how source effect and presentation effect interact, and indeed how the audience perceives and judges source and presentation in the context of the many signals or messages to which it is subjected in any single communications transaction.

The present research was not designed to answer these questions conclusively. But respondents were asked to react to a series of evaluation questions whose answers provide some clues. Specifically, these were questions designed to help indicate the relative weights which respondents assigned to source and to presentation in making their judgments and decisions. The results of three of these questions have already been discussed, specifically in the previous chapter's examination of an audience's trust of a source's product claims, its trust of a salesman, and its judgment about a salesman's product knowledge. The present chapter, following up on earlier clues on the possible power of presentation effect, looks at the results of a series of questions dealing very specifically with the salesman's activities as the audience perceived them within the context of what the message did and sought to do.

EVALUATION OF THE SALESMAN'S PRESENTATION

One of these questions required the audience to make a direct evaluation of the salesman's presentation. The question it was asked to answer was:

"Given the product and its expected use, was the sales engineer's presentation (check one):
   a. Good _____
   b. Average _____
   c. Poor _____"

The results are tabulated in Exhibit 6-1.

EXHIBIT 6-1

SOURCE, PRESENTATION, AND AUDIENCE EFFECTS INGREDIENTS: Evaluation of Sales Presentation, by Audience and by Source and Quality of Presentation *

Audience	Good Presentation			Poor Presentation		
	Mon-santo	Den-ver	Anony-mous	Mon-santo	Den-ver	Anony-mous
Purchasing Agents	1.3	1.2	1.0	1.8	1.7	1.9
Chemists	1.2	1.3	1.2	2.1	2.3	2.1
Students	1.4	1.5	1.3	2.5	1.9	1.9

* The scale is as follows:
   1 = Good
   2 = Average
   3 = Poor
Therefore the lower the number, the better the rating.

The best score it is possible to have in any one cell is 1.00. The worst score is 3.00. The results show that in 6 of 12 comparisons Denver and Anonymous (low-credibility sources) presentations were rated better than Monsanto (high-credibility source).[1] According to the binomial test, the probability that Monsanto ranks lower than the other two companies is not significant. But in 9 of 9 cases people seeing the good presentation rated it better than those seeing the poor one.[2] The level of statistical significance is 0.2%. And in 10 of 12 cases purchasing agents rated the presentations higher than chemists or students.[3] The level of statistical significance is 1.9%.

The 9 of 9 preference for the good presentation merely confirms the pre-test's findings of the soundness of the research instrument; namely that the "good" presentation, as perceived in the research design, was actually better than the "poor" presentation as perceived by the research subjects. The fact that in 10 of 12 cases purchasing agents gave the presentation more favorable ratings than chemists and students probably confirms earlier evidence that purchasing agents are either more responsive to or influenced by a good presentation. But by far the most interesting result of Exhibit 6-1 is the absence of any clear source-effect preference for Monsanto in these ratings. It will be recalled from Chapter 5 (Exhibit 5-12) that respondents generally ranked Monsanto salesmen's knowledge of the product they were selling below the Denver and Anonymous salesmen. Yet we now find them making no distinction between the quality of these company's salesmen's

---

[1] The twelve comparisons are as follows: 1.3 vs. 1.2 and 1.0; 1.2 vs. 1.3 and 1.2; 1.4 vs. 1.5 and 1.3; and 1.8 vs. 1.7 and 1.9; 2.1 vs. 2.3 and 2.1; and 2.5 vs. 1.9 and 1.9.

[2] The nine comparisons are as follows: 1.3 vs. 1.8; 1.2 vs. 2.1; and 1.4 vs. 2.5; 1.2 vs. 1.7; 1.3 vs. 2.3; and 1.5 vs. 1.9; 1.0 vs. 1.9; 1.2 vs. 2.1; and 1.3 vs. 1.9.

[3] The twelve comparisons are as follows: 1.3 vs. 1.2 and 1.4; 1.2 vs. 1.3 and 1.5; and 1.0 vs. 1.2 and 1.3; 1.8 vs. 2.1 and 2.5; 1.7 vs. 2.3 and 1.9; and 1.9 vs. 2.1 and 1.9.

presentations in support of the product. In Chapter 5 the uneven ranking of salesmen's product knowledge helped lead to the conclusion that industrial buyers have higher standards for the representatives of well-known companies than for those of less well-known companies. It suggested therefore that well-known companies must be more careful in selecting and training their representatives. This point also came out in Chapter 5 where it was shown (Exhibit 5-11) that respondents who chose to adopt the product under high-risk conditions generally rated the well-known company's salesmen as being less trustworthy than the salesmen of the other companies. For respondents who rejected the product, no such inverse source effect showed up in the trust ratings.

Whether this interpretation of the survey results—that is, the higher selection and training requisites of known companies—is correct is now thrown into question by the figures in Exhibit 6-1. The reason is that if the audience really has higher standards for the salesmen of a well-known company, in a straight scoring of these salesmen's presentations it would be expected to rate their presentations lower (less favorably) than those of the less well-known companies. But Exhibit 6-1 shows some ambiguity. Monsanto sales presentations were rated lower than Denver and Anonymous in six comparisons, higher in four, and tied in two. What is going on? Does the Chapter 5 interpretation of the higher selection and training requisites of known companies really hold up?

The answer depends on two things: (1) how do the source and presentation effects interact: how much does the favorable source effect which helps a well-known company, as a company, offset the inverse source effect which seems to hurt it via its salesmen, and (2) do lower presentation and trust scores for well-known companies actually indicate less favorable ratings, or could they, in fact, indicate more favorable ratings? The second question obviously needs to be answered first.

The result of the trustworthiness scores (Exhibit 5-11) are

capable of two opposing interpretations. Instead of suggesting that they *show* less trust in the well-known company's representatives, it could be argued that these scores merely show that a respondent requires himself to *have* less trust in a known company's salesmen in order to favor that company. He must have especially high trust in the salesman of a less well-known company in order to vote for that company. This argument would seem to be supported by the fact that neither a negative nor a positive source effect showed up among respondents who rejected the product when faced with a high-risk (adoption) question (Exhibit 5-11). This suggests that the lower trust ratings which the "yes" respondents gave to Monsanto salesmen under high-risk (adoption) decision situations were not a facilitating *cause* of their "yes" answers, but an *effect* of their greater confidence in Monsanto. This is especially suggested by their actual higher ratings of the reliability of Monsanto's product claims (see Exhibit 5-8). Since they trusted Monsanto and its products more, they did not have to trust its salesmen so much.

This leads directly into the question of the interaction between source and presentation effect. Exhibit 6-1 is based on a much less complex question than Exhibit 5-11. In the latter, in order to express his judgment about the trustworthiness of the salesman, the respondent was virtually forced to think in terms of the company the salesman represented. The reason this seems so is that one person (the respondent) was asked to make what was certainly a moral judgment about another person (the salesman). To make such a judgment created a difficult task for the respondent and placed him in a difficult situation. The reason is that trust in one's fellow man is a necessary condition of civilization. Without it there would be no society—only a world of tooth and claw. We are all dependent on the reliability of each other's word; and in a relatively few cases where that dependence is especially critical we legislate in order to assure this reliability and punish those who transgress against it. The requisite of trustworthiness, of a man being "as good as his word," is almost automatically understood by everybody as an essential ingredient of civilization. It is, in effect, a moral imperative. Hence, when the respondent was asked about the salesman's trustworthiness, he was in effect forced to make a profoundly moral judgment. Whether he was aware of that fact is less important than the great likelihood that in responding to the question, he probably automatically mustered all possible evidence before answering. The one single piece of evidence to distinguish one salesman from another (within each "quality-of-presentation" category; i.e., relatively good vs. relatively poor) was the company the salesman represented. Therefore the respondent's answer about the trustworthiness of the salesman must have been heavily conditioned by a similar judgment he was making about the company the salesman represented.

This suggests the very high probability that the results in Exhibit 5-11 contained a substantial quotient of source effect. The conclusion seems inescapable that the lower trust ratings of Monsanto salesmen are in effect little else than high ratings for Monsanto as a company. To this extent they are not really low trust ratings for Monsanto salesmen.

This conclusion seems thoroughly supported by the Exhibit 6-1 results, which required no moral judgment. The respondent was asked to rate not a man but a presentation. The respondent therefore was in a much more comfortable and neutral psychological position than he was in the question which produced Exhibit 5-11. Not only that, the question resulting in Exhibit 6-1 implied nothing, as some others did, regarding the wisdom of a respondent's previous product choice. When a respondent was asked about the trustworthiness of the salesman, about the reliability of the company, or about the salesman's competence to speak about the product, the respondent's answer to some extent must have contained an element of self-justification—an element to support his previous adoption decision. But when asked, as in connection with Exhibit 6-1, about the quality of the salesmen's presentation, there was much less need for self-justification in the response.

It would seem, therefore, that Exhibit 6-1 represents much more distinctly "clean" answers. Hence the failure of a source effect to have shown up in the respondents' reactions to the quality of the salesmen's presentations would seem to mean that the negative source effect suggested in Chapters 4 and 5 is a misnomer. It *looks* like a negative source effect, but it is really a positive source effect. It seems reasonable to conclude that what "looks" like negative source effect is really a measure of the extent to which the power of a company's favorable reputation reduces the amount of competence its salesmen (message transmitters) need in order for them to be effective. And it reduces the amount of trust the customer needs to have in these salesmen in order to accept their pleadings and the amount of self-confidence the customer needs in any decision he makes favorable to these salesmen's companies. Hence the salesmen of the well-known company do not seem to be disadvantaged by their company's reputations. On the contrary, they seem actually to be helped by these reputations.

In short, while the present research shows that the well-known company's salesmen were judged to have less product knowledge (see Exhibit 5-12), they were still trusted more and their company's products were still accepted more readily, in spite of the fact that the well-known company respondents scored no better and no worse than the others in their retention of the product information supplied by the salesmen (see Exhibit 5-14). This demonstrates the existence of a source effect that is much more complex than has been implied before. Moreover, to the extent that the suggested lesser product knowledge of the well-known company's salesmen may have reduced the respondents' willingness to adopt that company's product, the net result was still a higher proportion of adoptions for that company than for the less well-known companies. If indeed there was such a reduction, the higher adoption ratio suggests that source effect is even more powerful than a simple examination of the ratio itself implies.

It was also noted in Chapters 4 and 5 that the power of source effect is uneven as between the various audiences, and that chemists particularly were more inclined to favor the well-known company. But this does not show up in the audiences' evaluations of the sales presentation in Exhibit 6-1. That is, chemists favored the Monsanto sales presentations no more than did the other audiences. Therefore, the fact that they did, however, favor Monsanto in their actual product adoption decisions and in their self-confidence in these decisions seems to show that what really counted with them was the company's name or reputation and less how well the sales presentation communicated with them.

But this is not to suggest that they completely ignored presentation. Indeed, Exhibit 6-1 shows that the chemists were the most critical of poor presentations. Yet this did not prevent them from exceeding all others in the proportion of poor presentations whose products they adopted under high-risk decision conditions. Of those chemists who saw poor presentations, exactly 25% adopted the product under high-risk conditions, compared to 17.4% of the purchasing agents and 23.7% of the students. As noted in Chapters 4 and 5, chemists were somewhat less affected by presentation, and particularly a poor presentation, than were purchasing agents. When making a product choice, chemists seemed more likely to rely on their product competence than on the way in which that product was presented to them. Another and closely related interpretation is that chemists understood the presentation better than others, even when it was poor, and as a consequence remembered more information on the basis of which to make a judgment. (It will be recalled from Exhibit 5-14 that chemists generally retained more information from a poor presentation than purchasing agents did from a good one.) But in the process of being less adversely affected by a poor presentation, chemists were, slightly more than purchasing agents, influenced by the reputation of the company whose product they were judging (see Exhibit 4-6).

The net result of the various influences working on the decision-making process for each audience was that they seemed to cancel each other, as shown in Exhibit 6-2. The exhibit

EXHIBIT 6-2

RELATION OF PRESENTATION RATINGS TO AFFIRMATIVE DECISIONS: Percentage of Affirmative Decisions, by Presentation Ratings, Presentation Quality, and Audience, by Decision Situation

	Referral Decisions		Adoption Decisions	
Presentation Quality	"Good" Presentation Ratings	"Average" & "Poor" Presentation Ratings	"Good" Presentation Ratings	"Average" & "Poor" Presentation Ratings
	Purchasing Agents			
Good	90	80 *	40	50
Poor	90	62	32	7
Total	90	67	38	23
Combined total	81		34	
	Chemists			
Good	90	86	46	16
Poor	83	59	50 †	15
Total	89	73	47	16
Combined total	81		33	

* This means that of the purchasing agents who saw "good" presentations and rated these presentations as being either "average" or "poor," 80% said "yes," they would refer the product onward for further consideration.

† This means that of the chemists who saw "good" presentations and rated these presentations as being "good," 50% said "yes," they would directly adopt the product on their own initiative.

shows the percentages of affirmative responses to the two types of decision situations: referral and adoption situations. For each of these situations separate affirmative response ratios are presented for respondents who rated the presentations they saw as either "good," "average," or "poor." These categories are in turn separated by whether the quality of the presentation that was seen was either "good" or "poor." The resulting data show that while there were some differences between purchasing agents and chemists in some of the more detailed paired cells, on a consolidated basis there was almost no difference at all in the proportion of affirmative responses between purchasing agents and chemists. This was true regardless of the riskiness of the decision situation to which they responded; that is, referral or adoption. About a third of both groups took affirmative action under adoption situations, and exactly 81% of both took such action under referral situations.

Exhibit 6-2 also shows that when the influence of source is not specifically taken into account, the various audiences' feelings about the quality of the sales presentations (such as shown in Exhibit 6-1) are a poor predictor of purchasing behavior. There is, of course, no *prima facie* reason why, for example, a favorable presentation rating should predict favorable adoption action. A vote for the relative merits of the presentation could be a vote against the absolute merits of the product. But nonetheless it is interesting to know what, if any, relationship exists. Exhibit 6-2 shows that when an audience rates a presentation as being relatively above average, the proportion of affirmative responses under the higher-risk adoption situation is about the same for purchasing agents as for chemists. And while both their affirmative ratios decline when they rate the presentation as "average" or "poor," there is little difference in their respective affirmative ratios. To this extent it can be said that audience opinion regarding the quality of a sales presentation is a modestly good predictor of the referral action it will take, and, when not taking into account source influence, this predictor probably works equally well as between purchasing agents and the relatively more product-sophisticated technical personnel. A possible qualification to this generalization is that a low-presentation rating made by chemists may predict a somewhat lesser decline in the proportion of their affirmative referral actions than it does in the case of purchasing agents. Thus the average attrition for purchasing agents was 23% (90% — 67%), while for chemists it was only 16% (89% — 73%).

When it comes to the more risky adoption situation, the results of the experiment are much less clear-cut. The average affirmative response ratios are expectedly lower under adoption situations for both audiences. But there is a considerable difference between them on the predictive value of their presentation ratings. "Good" ratings by chemists are associated with a higher proportion of affirmative responses than are "good" ratings by purchasing agents (47% vs. 38%). On the other hand, chemists' "average" to "poor" ratings are associated with a lower portion of affirmative responses than are the same ratings by purchasing agents (16% vs. 23%). As a result, while under the less risky referral conditions chemists had a lesser affirmative attrition than purchasing agents as the presentation rating declined (16% vs. 23%), under the more risky adoption conditions they had a higher attrition (31% vs. 15%).

What all this suggests is that although what is perceived by the audience as a good sales presentation may result in more opinion change and more favorable (to the seller) purchasing behavior than one that is perceived as being less good, there are probably important differences between audiences, and between riskiness of the decisions they are making. Hence there are probably also important differences in the extent to which various audiences' evaluations of sales presentations indicate the likelihood of their recommending or buying the product that is presented to them.

The above conclusion raises questions about the relationship between the salesman's communications efforts and what he actually succeeded in communicating. To the degree that audiences differ in the extent to which their product choices can be somewhat predicted by their opinions of the sales presentation, is it because audiences differ in their *abilities* to understand and evaluate a product message, or in their *willingness* to evaluate the product, or in their *attitudes* toward salesmen? For example, it is reasonable to assume that the technical personnel ("chemists") were more competent than the purchasing agents to understand and judge the product. It has already been shown (see Exhibit 5-14) that they retained more of the transmitted information than did purchasing agents, and that this was probably due to their greater product competence. Did these differences in product competence influence the respective audiences' judgments about the quality of the sales presentation as the result of attitudes toward salesmen, regardless of audience product competence? Exhibit 6-3 helps

EXHIBIT 6-3

SOURCE, PRESENTATION, AND AUDIENCE EFFECTS INGREDIENTS:
Evaluation of Product Caliber Relative to Salesman's
Implication of Product Quality, by Audience
and Source and by Quality of Presentation *

	Good Presentation			Poor Presentation		
Audience	*Mon-santo*	*Den-ver*	*Anony-mous*	*Mon-santo*	*Den-ver*	*Anony-mous*
Purchasing Agents	1.9	2.1	2.1	2.1	2.4	2.4
Chemists	2.3	2.2	2.2	2.2	2.4	2.4
Students	2.1	2.1	2.2	2.2	2.1	2.2

* The scale is as follows:
  1 = The product is better than the sales engineer implied.
  2 = The product is as good as the sales engineer implied.
  3 = The product is not as good as the sales engineer implied.

answer this question. It is based on responses to the following question:

> "Which of the following opinions do you agree with most (check one only):
>   a. The product is better than the sales engineer implied _____.
>   b. The product is about as good as the sales engineer implied _____.
>   c. The product is not as good as the sales engineer implied _____."

For the most part purchasing agents judged the product, relative to what the salesman implied about it, about the same as chemists. Even though in four of six comparisons the purchasing agents' ratings were more favorable to the sales presentation than were the chemists' ratings, the actual differences between these ratings were too small to justify much confidence in generalizing on the four-in-six relationship. Thus in three of the four comparisons in which purchasing agents scored the presentations more favorably than the chemists, the differences were only 0.1; that is, from 2.1 to 2.2.

This means that the somewhat lower ratings chemists gave the presentations in Exhibit 6-1, especially on the poor presentations, must have been due primarily to the fact that chemists understood the product better than purchasing agents, not that they were in some way less tolerant or less understanding of salesmen, which is one way the results might have been interpreted in the absence of the product rating data. Exhibit 6-3 indicates that all audiences in all cells felt that the salesman was modestly inclined toward puffery. This is suggested from the fact that in 17 of the 18 cells the average ratings were 2.1 or above. If respondents had tended to think the salesman "undersold" the product, most of the averaged scores would have been 1.9 or less. To be between 2.0 and 3.0 suggests that respondents tended to believe the salesman "oversold." But interestingly, chemists felt hardly any stronger on this point than purchasing agents. However, since chemists were, in Exhibit 6-1, more inclined to the idea that the salesmen's presentations were not so good, this strongly suggests that it was their greater product knowledge that largely contributed to their less favorable reception of the salesmen's presentations, not any particular hostility toward or lack of respect or friendship for salesmen as a class.[4]

The above references to the predictive value of an audience's evaluation of a sales presentation are obviously hedged beyond the point of their having much value for the business firm. Few people would systematically want to set up the kinds of relationships discussed above to predict the sales consequences of various kinds of sales presentations. However, it is not uncommon for business executives to get exceedingly pleased and optimistic when a sales presentation is especially well received. The above findings suggest that in order to avoid false expectations and disappointments, it is useful to see that the relation between the likelihood of product adoption and audience evaluation of a presentation is a slight and tender one, and that in any case it varies considerably by the character of the customer and the riskiness of the decision he is required to make.

---

[4] The above reference to 17 of 18 ratings being 2.1 or above is not intended to suggest any statistical significance. A 2.1 rating, where 2.0 is average, and where each respondent can only vote "1," "2," or "3," is a trivial distinction. The point in citing the figure here is merely to see what inferences might be drawn and checked into. For example, it would seem reasonable for many persons to assume that chemists tend to rank salesmen relatively lower on the occupational status scale than purchasing agents would rate them. Hence, it would also seem reasonable to expect many people to interpret the chemists' tendencies to give sales presentations slightly lower ratings than would purchasing agents as merely reflecting the chemists' status bias. But with 17 of 18 ratings suggesting that the salesmen slightly exaggerated (or at least did not "soft-sell") the product's virtues, we have at least a strong implication that the chemists' feelings about the salesmen's status were no different from those of the other respondents.

All this is further supported by the answers to another evaluation question. Specifically, subjects were asked the following:

"Which of the following opinions do you agree with most (check one only):
  a. The quality of the sales presentation was better than the quality of the product itself _____.
  b. The quality of the sales presentation was about on par with the quality of the product itself _____.
  c. The quality of the sales presentation was worse than the quality of the product itself _____."

Exhibit 6-4 tabulates the results of this question. There is even less basis in this exhibit than in Exhibit 6-3 to suggest any relationship between respondents' relative evaluation of a product and a product presentation, on the one hand, and their willingness to adopt the product, on the other. The only thing that shows up in any clear fashion, as it did in the other exhibits in this chapter, is that a poor presentation always scores less well than a good one, regardless of the question that is asked.

EXHIBIT 6-4

SOURCE, PRESENTATION, AND AUDIENCE EFFECTS INGREDIENTS:
Evaluation of Sales Presentation Relative to the Product,
by Audience and Source, and by Quality
of Sales Presentation *

	Good Presentation			Poor Presentation		
Audience	Mon-santo	Den-ver	Anony-mous	Mon-santo	Den-ver	Anony-mous
Purchasing Agents	2.0	1.7	1.9	2.2	2.1	2.1
Chemists	1.7	2.0	1.8	2.2	2.3	2.3
Students	1.7	1.8	1.6	2.8	2.2	2.3

* The scale is as follows:
  1 = The presentation quality is better than the product quality.
  2 = The presentation quality is equal to the product quality.
  3 = The presentation quality is below the product quality.

The only other point that can be said to show up with some modest clarity is a substantiation of the earlier finding that technical personnel ("chemists") have a stronger source effect in favor of Monsanto than purchasing agents, and that in relating presentation quality to the source, purchasing agents exhibit the inverse source effect which so clearly validates the strength of the entire source effect hypothesis. Thus chemists gave lower scores (higher ratings) to the Monsanto presentation-product relationship than did either purchasing agents or students. They favored Monsanto, and purchasing agents, who were shown earlier to be more responsive to good presentations than to good names, favored the less well-known companies. These results do nothing more than confirm conclusions already reached, though based on different evidence.

EVALUATION OF THE SALESMAN'S FAMILIARITY WITH THE CUSTOMER'S PROBLEMS

If there is one tenet about the ingredients of sales effectiveness that dominates the modern rhetoric of industrial selling, it is that the salesman should know his customer and his customer's problems. This tenet represents a considerable change from the venerable admonition to the salesman, "Know your product." Now, although the importance of product knowledge is not denied, the prevailing theme is, "Know your customer."

The present research sought to determine which of these two tenets was more influential in obtaining product adoptions. Thus it asked respondents the following question:

"How well do you think the sales engineer knew the problems and operations of the company to which he was trying to sell? (Check one.)

    a. Very well _____
    b. Medium well _____
    c. Poorly _____"

Exhibit 6-5 shows the answers, rated on a three-point scale, with the lower scores representing the high ratings ("very well") and the higher scores the lower ratings ("poorly"). Exhibit 6-6 plots these scores against the proportion of product adoptions for each cell in Exhibit 6-5. The result shows a good relationship between the respondents' estimates of the salesman's familiarity with the problems and operations of the customer, and the respondents' ratio of adoptions. The more knowledgeable about the customer's problems the salesman was believed to be, the more the adoptions.

EXHIBIT 6-5

SOURCE, PRESENTATION, AND AUDIENCE EFFECTS INGREDIENTS:
Evaluation of Salesman's Familiarity with the Customer's
Problems, by Audience and Source, and by
Quality of Presentation *

	Good Presentation			Poor Presentation		
Audience	Mon-santo	Den-ver	Anony-mous	Mon-santo	Den-ver	Anony-mous
Purchasing Agents	1.3	1.3	1.1	2.4	2.0	2.1
Chemists	1.5	1.3	1.4	2.4	2.5	2.5
Students	1.4	1.3	1.3	2.5	2.9	2.1

* The scale is as follows:
  1 = Salesman was very well informed.
  2 = Salesman was medium well informed.
  3 = Salesman was poorly informed.

But it will be seen in Exhibit 6-6 that a second variable was really the more important one, namely, the quality of the sales presentation. The better the presentation, the better the respondents rated the salesman's familiarity with the customer's problems and the greater the ratio of adoptions. Since more of an effort was made in the good-presentation script to demonstrate the salesman's knowledge of his customer's problems and of his customer's interests and background, this result is not surprising.

EXHIBIT 6-6

"KNOW YOUR CUSTOMER": Relationship of Salesmen's Customer
Familiarity Rating Scores to Percentage of Adoptions,
Each Audience-Source Cell

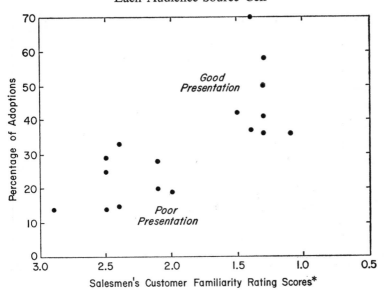

* The lower the score, the higher the familiarity rating; that is, 1 = high
familiarity, 3 = low familiarity.

Exhibit 6-7 makes for an interesting comparison. It plots
the ratio of adoptions against the respondents' ratings of the
salesmen's knowledge of the product they were selling. Thus
while Exhibit 6-6 looks at the "know your customer" slogan,
Exhibit 6-7 looks at "know your product." [5] Again the good
presentation gets both more adoptions and higher salesmen's
product knowledge ratings than the poor presentation. But
while there is more scatter in Exhibit 6-7 than in 6-6, there is
no indication that the "know your customer" admonition is
clearly more persuasive than that of "know your product."

---

[5] Based in part on Exhibit 5-12.

EXHIBIT 6-7

"KNOW YOUR PRODUCT": Relationship of Salesmen's Product
Knowledge Ratings to Percentage of Adoptions,
Each Audience-Source Cell

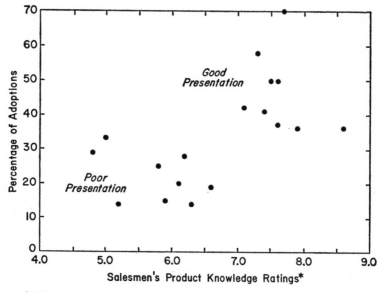

* The higher the rating, the greater the knowledge of the product.

With this said, a more realistic examination of Exhibits 6-6
and 6-7 does not improve things. What happens, for example,
if we eliminate student responses from these scatter diagrams
and identify purchasing agents and chemists separately? This
is done in Exhibits 6-8 and 6-9. The elimination of student responses, which presumably represent the least relevant responses from the point of view of experimental realism, does
nothing to alter the above conclusions. Exhibit 6-8, which is
the revised version of Exhibit 6-6, is no more revealing than
Exhibit 6-6. Each audience responds differently, showing once
again the great difficulty and high risk of generalization in this
area. The most that can be said is that Exhibit 6-8 ("know

EXHIBIT 6-8

"KNOW YOUR CUSTOMER": Relationship of Salesmen's Customer
Familiarity Rating Scores to Percentage of Adoptions,
Purchasing Agents and Chemists

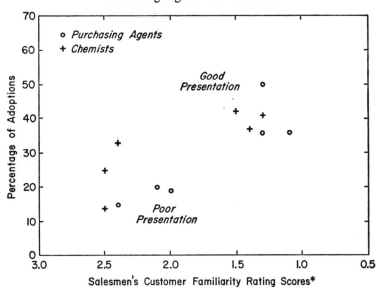

* The lower the score, the higher the familiarity rating.

your customer") has slightly less scatter on the horizontal scale
than does Exhibit 6-9 ("know your product"). In short, the
present research sheds no useful light on which of the above
two admonitions is right.

But source effect continues to show up, as Exhibit 6-5 indicates. The exhibit shows a modest inverse source effect, with
8 of 12 comparisons rating Monsanto salesmen's customer familiarity less favorably than Denver or Anonymous, for a
19.4% significance ratio according to the binomial test. The
lower rating of Monsanto salesmen indicates once again the
various audiences' higher expectations of the performance of
the well-known company's salesmen. But, at noted above, this

EXHIBIT 6-9

"KNOW YOUR PRODUCT": Relationship of Salesmen's Product
Knowledge Ratings to Percentage of Adoptions,
Purchasing Agents and Chemists

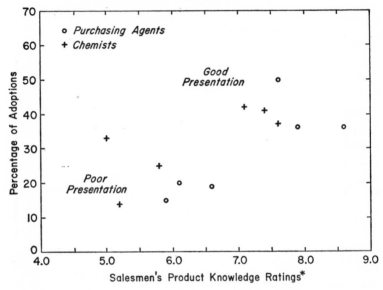

* The higher the rating, the greater the knowledge of the product.

does not appear to disable the favorably well-known company.
The power of such a company's credibility is so strong that, in
spite of lower ratings for its salesmen, the company's adoption
ratio is still disproportionately high.

CHAPTER 7

Interpretive Summary

CHAPTERS 4, 5, and 6 have examined source and sleeper effect from a variety of vantage points. The analysis has attempted to go several steps beyond most communications research in this general area. It has done this in part by a research instrument which distinguished between the "source" and the "communicator" of a message, by looking at the quality of the communication itself, by varying the competence of the respondents and the riskiness of the decisions they were asked to make, and by looking at a variety of respondent perceptions, such as the perceived trustworthiness of the source and of the communicator, the efficiency of the communication, the perceived competence of the communicator, and the respondent's confidence in his answers.

SOURCE, PRESENTATION, AUDIENCE, AND SLEEPER EFFECTS

As pointed out in Chapter 1, all experimental research suffers from the important limitation of being experimental. Its results should be generalized only with great care and with full awareness of the limitations imposed by the research design. In the case of the research reported in the previous chapters, one major thing seems to stand out clearly: regardless of how the experimental data were tabulated or analyzed, and regardless of how a variety of variables were either controlled or allowed to vary during the experiment, the research fully confirms the central theme of all published communications research; namely, source effect exercises a strong and abiding influence on audience decision making. It seems clearly to influence industrial purchasing situations that involve complex products in complex and costly operations. And it seems to operate whether the respondent's decision is a low-risk decision (say, recommending that the product get another hearing or a closer examination), or a high-risk decision (actually buying the product). In short, the results suggest that in terms of the effectiveness of an industrial products company's sales efforts, it always seems better for that company to be better-known rather than to be less well-known or anonymous. This is hardly a surprising finding. But it is also not a very useful finding.

Thus, the research found that the value of a company's general reputation is greatest when it is making efforts to get a first hearing for its product. To get it actually adopted (that is, for the respondent to make what is for him the high-risk decision of adoption rather than the lower-risk decision of recommending its further examination by his firm), the selling company's reputation does not produce as large a percentage of favorable audience responses as it does when the object is merely to get the prospect to give the product a favorable first hearing. In other words, the higher the riskiness of the decision the audience is asked to make, the less important is company reputation in influencing the audience. But a high-credibility reputation still produces more favorable responses under high-risk situations than a lower-credibility reputation.

What is essential therefore is to recognize the importance of audience risk-taking when talking about source effect. The riskiness of the decision the audience is expected to make affects its susceptibility to source effect. Thus, in the present research, on low-risk decisions (that is, on decisions merely to recommend further exploration of the product), while nine out of ten respondents acted favorably on the high-credibility company's presentation, less than eight out of ten acted favorably on the anonymous company's presentation. When respondents were put into a high-risk situation (having to decide themselves whether to adopt the product), the affirmative responses for the high-credibility company fell to 40% and for the anonymous company to 34%.

It was pointed out in Chapter 1 that only rarely do two different sources use the identical message in trying to influence an audience, and rarely do they use the identical presentation by an identical communicator. Yet much formal communications research has used identical messages, identical presentations, and identical communicators in a given experiment. Hence the question left unanswered by most of these studies of source effect is the extent to which message, presentation, and communicator differences can modify or even offset source influences. For example, is a poor presentation by a favorably well-known company as effective as a good presentation by a less well-known or anonymous company? Translated into commercial strategy, and assuming all other things equal, is it better for a company to spend more marketing money on mass media efforts to get itself well-known or on efforts to improve the direct presentations and the quality of its salesmen?

The present research demonstrates in a variety of ways that in the kind of situation it posed to its audiences, a good presentation produces a much greater favorable response than a poor one. And it has its greatest positive impact in high-risk situations; that is, when respondents are asked to take full personal responsibility for product adoption decisions rather than merely recommending further hearings for the product. In short, a good presentation always helps, but helps much more to get product adoption than just to get a favorable first hearing. Thus the minimum that can be said is that it clearly pays to get the best presentations and "presenters" to those meetings or sales situations at which decision makers are present: to marshal the best men for the crucial situations.

But the results vary considerably by source reputation. A

high-credibility source is at a powerful advantage, particularly in getting an initial favorable response (that is, in low-risk decision situations). Thus, the research shows that to get a favorable first hearing, a relatively *poor* presentation (but not one that is obviously bad) by a well-known company is about as effective as a relatively *good* presentation (but not one that is obviously superb) by an anonymous one. In short, for getting favorable low-risk decisions, there appears to be a simple trade-off between more and better advertising vs. more and better sales presentations and salesmen training. But to get favorable action in high-risk decision-making situations, a *poor* presentation by a well-known company may be less effective than a *good* one by an anonymous company. Conversely, a good presentation by an anonymous company is much better than a poor one by a well-known company. Hence, presentation quality can be a powerful neutralizer of the obvious power of source effect. Given the structure of the present research design, in which company reputation was paired against a simulated face-to-face confrontation between the salesman and the customer (audience), it can be said that in the final decision-making (purchase resolution) situation, the quality of the face-to-face presentation is more important in getting product adoption than advertising or public relations efforts designed to raise the source's (company's) generalized reputation.

While a good presentation by a high-credibility company always scored better than a good one by a low-credibility company, the results are also conclusive in showing that in all situations a poor presentation resulted in substantially lower sales (persuasive) effectiveness. However, to get an initial favorable hearing (low-risk decision), a better message, and a better presentation of that message, by a medium- or low-reputation source seems to have been slightly better than a poor message and poor presentation by a high-reputation source. For high-risk decisions (to get product adoption), better messages and better presentations by a low-reputation source were strongly superior to poor messages and poor presentations by a high-reputation source. Translated into operating marketing strategies, this means that when a low-reputation company uses more effectively prepared sales messages and trains its salesmen better, the combined effect of these efforts can be to wipe out what would otherwise have been an automatic advantage bestowed on a company with a good general reputation.

In summary, as applied at least to industrial purchasing situations of the type posed in the present experiment, it seems clear that the generalized conclusions of most source effect studies might very usefully be expanded to include considerations relating to the audience and the message. When faced with greater risk in connection with the opinions or actions advocated by the source, the audience greatly reduces its willingness to move toward those opinions or actions. Moreover, when it does move in the directions advocated by the source, in the present research it was found to rely more heavily on the quality of the message and its presentation than on the source's reputation.

Clearly, the audience is not a passive consumer of communications. It exercises a certain kind of initiative of its own, choosing in some circumstances to accept and in others to reject the communicator's pleas and blandishments. Whether he does one or the other has a great deal to do with what is at stake, with the riskiness of the decision in question. Hence for some purposes a source's reputation for credibility may influence an audience and for other purposes it may not.

The question now remains how audience (customer) decisions varied by the competence or sophistication of the audience. Perhaps the most striking result involved the decisions of technical personnel. As a group, they were substantially more sophisticated about the kind of product that was presented in the experiment than were either purchasing agents or students. Hence one would generally have expected their decisions to be least affected by either the source's reputation, the quality of the message and its presentation, or the riskiness of the required decision. The experimental results are surprisingly unexpected.

Technical personnel demonstrated considerably more susceptibility to source effect than might ordinarily be expected. First of all, all three audiences displayed a source effect preference for the high-credibility company under low-risk conditions. Moreover, each audience substantially reduced its proportion of affirmative responses when put into the high-risk position of deciding whether actually to adopt the product. But under these high-risk conditions, the technically more sophisticated audience displayed a considerably greater susceptibility to the more prestigious company than the technically less sophisticated audience. In other words, in precisely the situation where there was most at stake and where technical sophistication most clearly helped those who had it, those who had it seemed to rely on it less and were more inclined than those who did not have it to rely on source prestige to make their decisions. This finding is contrary to the widely held assumption in the business community that the greater the customer's product sophistication or competence, the less he is influenced by the seller's reputation.

The present research suggests that when it comes to making final purchasing decisions the opposite may be true, at least as it relates to technical personnel versus purchasing agents. Why? Why, in the high-risk situation, did the technically less sophisticated purchasing agents seem to discount the reputation of the seller (source) more than the technically more sophisticated respondents?

The answer may very well be less a function of the different degrees of audience product sophistication than of audience purchasing sophistication. Purchasing agents talk with salesmen numerous times each day. They learn to deal with salesmen and the companies they represent. They are presented with numerous new products all the time. But in the case of highly technical products of the kind presented in the film, purchasing agents seldom make the final product adoption decisions. Chemists more often do. Yet purchasing agents must screen these and other product presentations daily. Hence they may, in effect, use the reputation of a company as a screening device to help them determine whether a product should get a further hearing. But when it comes to a high-risk adoption decision the very fact of their lesser product sophistication may cause them to be especially careful about using the same high-source reputation as a way of making such an important decision. Since they will have had more unpleasant experiences in such decisions—more experiences of a decision that turned out bad—they are more careful and discount the reputation of the selling company more than do less experienced purchasers. To the extent this analysis is true, it is not the greater *product* sophistication of the chemists which produces in them more source effect, but the greater *purchasing* sophistication of the purchasing agents that produces in them relatively less source effect. The sophistication that counts is perhaps not product sophistication but purchasing sophistication, at least in the high-risk adoption decision.

Finally, the experiment found that technical personnel are to a surprising extent influenced by the quality of both the sales presentation and the sales message. The better the message and its presentation, the greater their affirmative responses. But interestingly, message and presentation effect seemed to be most powerful in the low-risk situations. All other things being equal, the riskier the situation, the less powerfully technical personnel were influenced by message or presentation quality, even though source prestige influenced them considerably.

Purchasing agents were also affected by message and presentation quality. However, contrary to chemists, the presentation effect influenced them more in high-risk situations than in low-risk situations. But the apparent pattern of influence was more along the lines of a poor presentation hurting a company's standing with the purchasing agent than a good one helping it.

In any case, regardless of the audience involved or the riskiness of the decision, the role of message and presentation quality cannot be ignored. And the more risky the decision, the more important the role of presentation. The study results show that in higher-risk situations, regardless of the audience, any good presentation by any less well-known company always outperformed all poor presentations of any well-known company. When it came to making an actual sale (or achieving the final decisive influence that produced the desired concrete results), there was no substitute for a good, well-presented message, regardless of the audience or the source's reputation (credibility).

The present research uncovered the same kind of sleeper effect other communications researchers have found. That is, the favorable influence of source effect declined with the passage of time such that the proportion of respondents reacting favorably to the original presentations rose for the less well-known sources and fell for the well-known source. But there were several surprises of particular interest to the business community. For example, respondents who made either a strong or even partial gesture toward accepting the product immediately after seeing the filmed sales presentation, exhibited a five-week follow-up or sleeper attrition in inverse proportion to the intensity of their original convictions in support of the product. The stronger the original support, the less the subsequent attrition. This suggests the very common-sense notion that a simple look at the original responses to the original message is not really enough of a basis for predicting the duration of people's opinions (or actions) over time. It is useful to look at the strength of the original convictions. What is surprising, however, was the finding that looking at the strength of convictions in this way holds only for positive convictions.

Among respondents who completely and strongly rejected the original sales approach at the time of their viewing, there was a strong tendency five weeks later to give it another hearing. While all three audiences suffered from a form of cognitive dissonance which seemed to have caused them to change their minds in subsequent interviews, persons who were most certain about fully rejecting the product at first seemed most bothered later by their original decisions and seemed most likely to reverse them. They seemed, in short, more susceptible to subsequent efforts to get them to reconsider than were persons who vacillated in their original responses. This suggests that follow-up sales calls designed to get people to change their minds may be more effective with strong rejections of the original call than with vacillating rejections of such calls.

Good presentations also proved more effective than poor ones in the durability of their favorable influences on respondents. Moreover, good presentations by less well-known companies proved more durably effective than poor presentations by well-known companies.

The repeated evidence of the power of presentation effect in the communications process, and of the powerful role of audience competence and audience viewpoints, suggests that both communications researchers and business practitioners would be well advised to examine the concept of source effect with a more critical eye on its components and the variables that impinge upon them. The influence of source effect varies by the audience, with different audiences exercising different degrees and kinds of "initiative," to use Bauer's concept of "the obstinate audience."

Since business firms, governments, and other groups compete for various audiences' support and attention vis-à-vis their respective competitors in ways that use different messages and different ways of presenting them, it is clear that none of them can afford to let themselves be guided exclusively by communications literature which emphasizes the power of source ef-

fect to the exclusion of presentation effect. Indeed, the present
research contains evidence to suggest that while source effect
is extremely powerful, some influential studies have unintentionally exaggerated the power of this influence by acciden-
tally counting presentation effect as part of source effect. This
is discussed in detail in Chapter 5.

THE ROLES OF SELF-CONFIDENCE, TRUST, RISK, AND INFORMATION
    RETENTION

Cox has demonstrated [1] in connection with women's evaluations of nylon stockings that their generalized confidence in
themselves and in their ability to evaluate a particular product
affects their persuasibility. In the present research, whenever
respondents were asked to make a decision they were immediately required to indicate the strength of their convictions in-
cident to these decisions. The results showed that in low-risk
decisions there was little difference in the degrees of confidence
expressed as between affirmative and negative decisions. While
in high-risk situations the confidence levels of respondent decisions tended to be relatively low, respondents were considerably more confident about their negative (would not adopt the
product) decisions than their affirmative decisions. Hence,
the more the personal risk, the more persuasion it takes to get
the customer (audience) to switch his allegiance to a given
product (opinion). In terms of risk analysis, the more the personal risk, the more confident the customer (audience) is that
it is less risky not to change from a given product (or opinion) than to change. Once the customer (audience) has made
a decision in a high-risk situation, the seller (communicator)
has greater difficulty both in getting the negative respondent to
change his mind and in keeping the affirmative respondent
from changing his mind. As between these two categories of

[1] Donald F. Cox, *Information and Uncertainty: Their Effects on Consumers' Product Evaluations,* 1962.

respondents, the affirmative ones were found to be somewhat less sure of themselves than the negative ones.

To the extent that these findings can be applied to commercial situations, they suggest that in switching a customer to one's product, the more that can be done to reassure him he has made the right choice, the less his susceptibility to the counterpersuasion of a competing product.

The power of source effect again showed up with great force in the analysis of respondent confidence scores. The decision-confidence scores of affirmative respondents to the high-credibility source were clearly lower than those of the lower-credibility sources. This indicates that the high-credibility source did not require as much self-confidence on the part of respondents for them to favor that source. Confidence in the source reduced the need for the respondent to have a lot of confidence in his own judgment. Conversely, the respondent *had* to have more confidence in his response in order to *reject* the high-credibility source than he needed to reject the lower-credibility source. Thus in the kind of situation tested in the present research, it appears that the well-known company seems to be better insulated, not only against the probability of negative responses, but also against counterpersuasion in respect to affirmative responses. This seems to be particularly true of chemists as compared to purchasing agents, and helps confirm other findings that purchasing agents were not as much affected by company reputation. But the results showed again that purchasing agents were more affected by message presentation.

Regarding sleeper effect, the usual research findings were confirmed insofar as they apply to respondent confidence scores. Responses to high-credibility sources showed a lower drop in self-confidence follow-up scores than responses to the lower-credibility sources. Moreover, in the low-risk situations, respondents who answered affirmatively in both the original questionnaire and in the follow-up had reduced self-confidence scores in the latter. But the original affirmative respondents who answered negatively on the follow-up had higher follow-up confidence scores.

What is perhaps more significant, however, is the effect of presentation quality. The results showed a definite positive sleeper effect in connection with presentation quality. Persons who originally saw good presentations always had a rise in their follow-up confidence scores, while those who originally saw poor presentations generally had a follow-up drop. That is, the confidence-producing effect of a good presentation improved with the passage of time, as did the confidence-detracting effect of a poor presentation. The advantages of a good presentation over a poor one tended to grow and become strengthened over time.

The net result of all this says, in effect, that sleeper effect, as expected, works "against" a high-credibility source but, unexpectedly, it works "for" a well-presented message. That is, the advantages of a good sales presentation are more durable than those of a good generalized reputation by its source. As source effect wears off, the greater durability of the message results in a rise in the relative importance of the message effect. Still, the absolute ratio of favorable responses on follow-up decisions were more favorably related to source reputation than to presentation quality. The power of source effect stands out undiminished.

Hovland, Weiss, Kelman, and others have found that source effect is basically a function of the perceived trustworthiness of the source. The present research fully confirms this conclusion as it applies to the kind of industrial purchasing situation that was examined. Respondents gave the high-credibility source significantly higher "trustworthiness" ratings than the low-credibility sources.

However, analysis in Chapter 6 shows that when they rated the trustworthiness of the company high, they tended to rate the trustworthiness of its salesmen low. This is apparently a manifestation of the double-edged character of source effect. It can strike both "for" and "against" the high-credibility company. What apparently happens is that when the credibility of a company (source) is high, the customer (audience) has higher expectations regarding that company's performance and the performance of its representatives. In view of the fact that the research also showed a very considerable relationship between customer trust in the salesman and the proportion of favorable (to the source) actions by the customer, this offhand would seem to suggest that the high-credibility company has a special need to make special efforts to upgrade and sustain a high level of performance by its salesmen. A good company reputation, regardless of how it was obtained, can be diluted and destroyed in a number of ways. But the above findings suggest that the more successful a company is in building that reputation by ways other than those involving its salesmen, the harder it is obliged to work at developing customer trust in its salesmen if its reputation is to pay off fully.

While this conclusion seems plausible enough, other data from the present research suggest another possibility. It was found that while respondents ranked the product knowledge (or competence) and trustworthiness of salesmen from the prestigious company lower than they ranked salesmen from other companies, they still preferred the product of the former company. Regardless of how poorly they thought of the prestigious company's salesmen, they still preferred doing business with that company.

This and a variety of other data suggest that instead of meaning that the lower trust ratings of the high-credibility company salesmen *show* less trust in the well-known company's representatives, they actually show that a respondent required himself to *have* less trust in a known company's salesmen in order to favor that company. Conversely, the respondent was required to have had especially high trust in the salesmen of a less well-known company in order to vote for that

company's products. Thus the lower trust and knowledge ratings of the high-credibility company's salesmen was actually an
effect of the respondents' greater confidence in the high-credibility *company,* not an indication that respondents set higher
standards for the salesmen of the high-credibility company.
Since they trusted the source more, they did not have to trust
its representatives as much. Hence what, in the previous discussion, "looked" like a negative source effect—a high source
reputation striking "against" the representatives of that source
—was actually a measure of the extent to which the power of a
source's favorable reputation reduced, in the minds of respondents, the amount of competence and trustworthiness its
representatives (message transmitters) needed in order for
them to be effective. The representatives (salesmen) of the
well-known company were not disadvantaged by their company's reputation. They were greatly helped by its reputation.

This strongly suggests that it clearly pays for the company
to build a strong reputation, or at least get itself favorably
well-known. It would also seem that the salesmen of the less
well-known companies labor under the great disadvantage of
perhaps having to seem much more knowledgeable and trustworthy than those of the known company. Put another way,
the favorably well-known company may be in the felicitous
position of actually being able to afford to have less "trustworthy" salesmen. However, in the long run this might damage the reputation of the company itself. What can be said is
this: in the short run, to the extent that a company's favorably
well-known reputation is created by things other than the behavior, practices, and personalities of its salesmen, that reputation apparently puts such a company's "poor" salesmen at
somewhat of an advantage over a less well-known company's
"good" salesmen when introducing new products.

All this testifies to the enormous power of source effect in
industrial purchasing situations. But it also raises questions
about the completeness or thoroughness of certain aspects of

experimental communications research. As noted above, the present research has revealed a tendency for respondents who rated a high-credibility source (company) high in trustworthiness to rate its representatives (salesmen) low in trustworthiness. In the present research the salesman was the medium through which the source spoke. The presence of such a middleman is the typical case in mass communication. But if communications research has generally found that high-credibility sources are generally rated high in trustworthiness, this means that such research must generally have had the source speak for himself rather than through a middleman. An examination of the research instruments that were used indicates that this has indeed been the typical situation.

Persons and organizations engaged in mass communication must therefore take careful note of the role of the intermediary in designing their programs. If the intermediary—the presenter of the message—is low in perceived trustworthiness, over the long run he can damage the cause of the high-credibility source. And the higher the perceived credibility of the source, in the long run the higher must be the perceived trustworthiness of its message transmitter or communicator in order to prevent his detracting from the source's effectiveness.

The world of advertising in part recognizes the power of the intermediary. Certain television performers and announcers, for example, are in great demand because advertisers and their agencies believe the public thinks of these persons as very "honest," "reliable," and "sincere." What these advertisers and agencies seem not to have been fully aware of is the possibility that the more credible the public perceives a company (source) to be, the more "honest," "reliable," and "sincere" it apparently "requires" that company's representatives to be.

Finally, the present research indicates that the perceived trustworthiness of the communicator was not as closely related to the audience's feelings about the communicator's knowledge or understanding of the product he was selling as might be supposed. It was much more closely related to the quality of his sales presentation. The better the presentation, the more trustworthy the salesman was perceived to be. And the higher the score, the more favorably respondents reacted to his product. What this means is that there was an unexpectedly high presentation effect, and the way it was found to play back on the source may require communications research to give attention to the possibility that what has been called source effect contains a substantial element of presentation effect.

A poor presentation reduced trust in the source, but it reduced trust in the message transmitter even more. Interestingly, however, this varied with the audience. Chemists particularly downgraded the salesman. Beyond that, they strongly tended to perceive a poor presentation as being the fault of the message transmitter and not the company he represented. They tended to protect the company and blame the salesman when they saw a poor presentation. This was not the case with purchasing agents, which further emphasizes how much chemists were subject to source effect.

Exactly what constitutes "poorness" in a presentation is not clear. What is clear is that it is more than a single element. What is said by the communicator, how he says it, and his personality are all factors. "Poorness" is a multidimensional quantity in presentation just as "credibility" seems to be multidimensional in the concept of source effect.

It was noted above that there was no clear relationship between an audience's rating of a salesman's trustworthiness and its judgment regarding the extent of his knowledge or understanding of the product he was selling. Perhaps more significant was that the audience's willingness to recommend or adopt the product was also not clearly related to its judgment about the salesman's product knowledge. Clearly the audience, in making its adoption decisions, was influenced by more than what the salesman specifically said about the product. It seems reasonable to assume that elements of personality and what he said other than about the product and its uses played an important role in influencing the audience.

As in the case of trustworthiness ratings, the higher the credibility of the source, the lower the audience perceived the salesman's product knowledge to be. Yet in spite of all this, regardless of how the data were tabulated and separated, the high-credibility source always had the highest proportion of favorable audience responses to its product. Thus, neither a lower salesman's product-knowledge rating, nor a lower salesman's trust rating, prevented the respondent from more frequently adopting the product of the high-credibility company which the salesman represented. This suggests either that the sales producing (or persuasive) power of a high-credibility source was enormous, or that there was a reverse source effect which caused respondents to downgrade representatives of well-known companies (sources) because they had higher levels of expectations regarding the performances of these representatives. While there is no doubt about the power of source effect, the latter explanation was found to be the more plausible.

Finally, the research showed that an audience's judgment about a salesman's product knowledge was not related to the amount of information the salesman succeeded in communicating to the audience. Thus the audience made its judgment about the salesman's knowledge on something different from the knowledge he successfully transmitted to the audience. Moreover, the amount of knowledge transmitted had little bearing on whether the audience would react favorably toward the source in its buying decisions. What did happen, however, was that more effective product-knowledge transmission at the outset tended to produce more durable product adoption decisions. Thus, persons who retained more of the transmitted information at the time of the sales communication tended to be more steadfast in their affirmative decisions over time. This was not as true of persons who rejected the product at the outset. Thus the power of sleeper effect which results in a change of the original favorable opinion or action with the passage of time was moderated in some proportion related to how much information about the product the respondent retained in the first place. People who were originally influenced in the direction advocated by the source were more likely to stay influenced as they retained more of the product information (facts) that they originally had. Therefore, in the long run it is well for the source to work hard at getting his facts across. This means, of course, working hard on the presentation.

* * * * *

The over-all summary of this research therefore is as follows:

1. The existence of source and sleeper effect seems to be confirmed in industrial purchasing situations.
2. However, their effect varies by the competence and sophistication of the audience, and in some rather unexpected ways.
3. They are also moderated by the power of message and presentation effect.
4. Generally speaking, it pays to have a good company reputation.
5. But an anonymous (perhaps new) company can in part overcome the advantage of a high-credibility competitor by superior sales messages and superior salesmen.
6. Still, the power of source effect is so strong that a poor presentation by a high-credibility company can still compete very effectively with a good presentation of a low-credibility company.
7. But a good presentation by itself is extremely powerful, and capable of overcoming some of the obvious disadvantages of its being made by a representative of a low-credibility source.
8. The power of source effect and of presentation effect varies by the audience and by the riskiness of the decisions the audience is expected to make. Thus, the greater the risk, the

less powerful is source effect and the more powerful is presentation effect.

9. Communications research may not have adequately distinguished between the message source and the message communicator, with the result that the commercial user of this research can be seriously misled if he is not careful to understand the power of the distinction.

10. Presentation effect, message effect, and audience effect appear to be powerful components in the communications mix and need much more careful study than they have received.

11. However, there is strong indication that measurements of these effects, when they are based on induced changes in audience opinions, may not be very good indicators of probable changes in audience actions. There appears to be a big gap between indicated opinion change and public action change.

12. To the extent that much experimental communications research has employed college students as subjects, the present research indicates the need for extreme care in generalizing from the responses of these subjects. In the present research there were often great differences between student responses and the responses of operating business personnel.

Bibliography

Bauer, Raymond A., "Communication as a Transaction," *Public Opinion Quarterly,* Vol. 27, No. 1, Spring 1963, pp. 83–86.

——, "The Communicator and the Audience," *Journal of Conflict Resolution,* Vol. 2, No. 1, March 1958, pp. 66–77.

——, "Consumer Behavior as Risk-Taking," in Robert S. Hancock, ed., *Dynamics Marketing in a Changing World,* Proceedings of the 43rd National Conference, American Marketing Association, June 1960.

——, "The Obstinate Audience," *American Psychologist,* Vol. 19, No. 5, May 1964, pp. 319–328.

——, "Risk Handling in Drug Adoption: The Role of Company Preference," *Public Opinion Quarterly,* Vol. 25, No. 4, Winter 1961, pp. 546–559.

Bowden, A. O., Floyd F. Caldwell, and Guy A. West, "A Study in Prestige," *American Journal of Sociology,* Vol. 40, No. 4, September 1934, pp. 193–203.

Brown, Arthur A., Frank T. Hulswit, and John D. Kettelle, "A Study of Sales Operations," *Operations Research,* Vol. 4, No. 3, June 1956, pp. 296–308.

Cox, Donald F., *Information and Uncertainty: Their Effects on Consumers' Product Evaluations.* Boston: Harvard Business School, 1962, unpublished doctoral dissertation.

DeWolf, John W., "A New Tool for Setting and Selling the Advertising Budget," speech before the Eastern Regional Meeting, American Association of Advertising Agencies, November 7, 1963.

Dietze, Alfred G., and George E. Jones, "Factual Memory of Secondary School Pupils for a Short Article Which They Read a

Single Time," *Journal of Educational Psychology,* Vol. 22, No. 8, November 1931, pp. 586–598, and Vol. 22, No. 9, December 1931, pp. 667–676.

Dowst, Somerby, "How Purchasing Agents Are Rating You," *Sales Management,* June 19, 1964, pp. 30–32.

England, Wilbur B., *Procurement: Principles and Cases.* Homewood, Illinois: Richard D. Irwin, Inc., 4th ed., 1962.

Festinger, Leon, *A Theory of Cognitive Dissonance.* Evanston, Illinois: Row, Peterson, 1957.

Hilibrand, Murray, *Source Credibility and the Persuasive Process.* Boston: Harvard Business School, 1964, unpublished doctoral dissertation.

Hovland, Carl I., "Changes in Attitude Through Communication," *Journal of Abnormal and Social Psychology,* Vol. 46, No. 3, July 1951, pp. 424–437.

——, Irving L. Janis, and Harold H. Kelley, *Communication and Persuasion.* New Haven: Yale University Press, 1953.

——, Arthur A. Lumsdaine, and Fred D. Sheffield, *Experiments in Mass Communication.* Princeton: Princeton University Press, 1949.

——, and Walter Weiss, "The Influence of Source Credibility on Communication Effectiveness," *Public Opinion Quarterly,* Vol. 15, No. 4, Winter 1951–1952, pp. 635–650.

How Industry Buys. New York: Scientific American, Inc., 1955.

Janis, Irving L., "Personality Correlates of Susceptibility to Persuasion," *Journal of Personality,* Vol. 22, No. 4, June 1954, pp. 504–518.

——, and Seymour Feshback, "Personality Differences Associated with Responsiveness to Fear-Arousing Communications," *Journal of Personality,* Vol. 23, No. 2, December 1954, pp. 154–166.

Kelman, Herbert C., and Carl I. Hovland, " 'Reinstatement' of the Communicator in Delayed Measurement of Opinion Change," *Journal of Abnormal and Social Psychology,* Vol. 48, No. 3, July 1953, pp. 327–335.

Klopper, Joseph, *The Effect of Mass Communication.* Glencoe, Illinois: The Free Press, 1960.

Kulp, Daniel H., II, "Prestige, as Measured by Single-Experience

Changes and Their Permanency," *Journal of Educational Research*, Vol. 27, No. 9, May 1934, pp. 663–672.

Maccoby, Nathan and Eleanor E., "Homeostatic Theory in Attitude Change," *Public Opinion Quarterly*, Vol. 25, No. 4, Winter 1961, pp. 537–545.

Magee, John F., "Operations Research in Making Marketing Decisions," *Journal of Marketing*, Vol. 25, No. 2, October 1960, pp. 18–23.

——, "Some Approaches to Measuring Marketing Results," *Proceedings of the National Conference, American Marketing Association*, Philadelphia, December 1957.

McGraw-Hill Publishing Company, *How Advertising Affects the Cost of Selling*. New York: McGraw-Hill, 1963.

National Association of Purchasing Agents, *Evaluation of Supplier Performance*. New York: The Association, 1963.

Rarick, Galen R., "Effects of Two Components of Communicator Prestige," unpublished paper presented at the Pacific Chapter, American Association of Public Opinion Research, Asilomar, California, January 25, 1963.

Saadi, Mitchel, and Paul R. Farnsworth, "The Degrees of Acceptance of Dogmatic Statements and Preferences for Their Supposed Makers," *Journal of Abnormal and Social Psychology*, Vol. 29, No. 2, July–September 1934, pp. 143–150.

Sawyer, Howard G., "How to Use Emotional Factors in Your Advertising to Metalworking," in F. Robert Shoaf, *Emotional Factors Underlying Industrial Purchasing*.

Schlaifer, Robert, *Introduction to Statistics for Business Decisions*. New York: McGraw-Hill Book Company, 1961.

Shoaf, F. Robert, *Emotional Factors Underyling Industrial Purchasing*. Cleveland: Steel (Penton Publishing Company), 1959.

Vidale, M. L., and H. B. Wolfe, "An Operations Research Study of Sales Response to Advertising," *Operations Research*, Vol. 5, No. 3, June 1957, pp. 370–381.

Webster, Frederick E., *Modeling the Industrial Buying Process*. New York: Graduate School of Business, Columbia University, 1964, unpublished paper.

Weiss, Walter, "A 'Sleeper' Effect in Opinion Change," *Journal of Abnormal and Social Psychology,* Vol. 48, No. 2, April 1953, pp. 173–180.

Westing, John H., and Isidor V. Fine, *Industrial Purchasing.* New York: John Wiley and Sons, 2nd ed., 1961.